A Classroom Teacher's Guide to Struggling Writers

How to Provide Differentiated Support and Ongoing Assessment

Curt Dudley-Marling
and
Patricia C. Paugh

HEINEMANN
Portsmouth, NH

Heinemann
361 Hanover Street
Portsmouth, NH 03801–3912
www.heinemann.com

Offices and agents throughout the world

The authors and publisher wish to thank those who have generously given permission to reprint borrowed material:

Excerpt from *Snakes* by Michele Dufresne. Copyright © 2007 by Michele Dufresne. Published by Pioneer Valley Education Press. Reprinted by permission of the publisher.

Library of Congress Cataloging-in-Publication Data
Dudley-Marling, Curt.
   A classroom teacher's guide to struggling writers : how to provide differentiated support and ongoing assessment / Curt Dudley-Marling, Patricia C. Paugh.
       p. cm.
   Includes bibliographical references and index.
   ISBN-13: 978-0-325-00765-6
   ISBN-10: 0-325-00765-9
   1. English language—Composition and exercises—Study and teaching (Elementary). 2. Language arts—Remedial teaching. I. Paugh, Patricia C. II. Title.
LB1576.D824 2009
372.62'3—dc22   2009007078

Editor: Kate Montgomery
Production: Elizabeth Valway
Cover design: Joni Doherty
Composition: Achorn International
Manufacturing: Steve Bernier

Printed in the United States of America on acid-free paper
13 12 11 10 09   VP   1 2 3 4 5

Contents

Acknowledgments

We wish to acknowledge Mary Moran and Mary Hamilton from the Boston Massachusetts Public Schools, and Kim Still Gilbert and Patricia O'Malley from the Springfield Massachusetts Public Schools, for contributing their work to this book. In addition we acknowledge Rebecca McKay from the Cornerstone Initiative for supporting the analysis of classroom work included in this book.

Teaching Struggling Writers

Some Underlying Principles

Learning to produce written language effectively is among the important achievements of a developing person, whether that person is a child at an early stage of learning to write or an adult struggling with similar aspects of the process.
> —J. Newman, "On Becoming a Writer," 1983, 860

Thanks largely to the groundbreaking work of Donald Graves and Lucy Calkins, their students, and their colleagues, the teaching of writing enjoys a prominent place in many elementary classrooms. Key elements of writing workshop—minilessons, conferences, revision, published work, student ownership—influence the teaching of writing in elementary classrooms across the English-speaking world and are backed by the support of a significant body of theory and research (e.g., Britton et al. 1975; Emig 1971; Farnan and Dahl 2003; Graves 1983; Hoewisch 2001; National Center for Educational Statistics 2002; Perry and Drummond 2002; Shaughnessy 1977). Practitioner journals such as *Language Arts* and *The Reading Teacher* regularly feature articles, sometimes entire issues, on the teaching of writing. Similarly, professional books and videos on the teaching of writing continue to be popular with teachers. Yet there is widespread concern that the national obsession with early reading instruction may be squeezing writing out of many elementary classrooms (Manzo 2003). There is also evidence that many teachers are being pressured to teach writing as it is assessed on high-stakes tests, with the result that in some classrooms writing instruction has been reduced to practicing timed responses to various writing prompts.

It is also noteworthy that, compared to the needs of struggling readers, the needs of struggling writers have received relatively little attention in the educational literature. This dearth of guidance for classroom teachers who work with struggling writers inspired us to write this book, which complements our earlier text on struggling readers, *A Classroom Teacher's Guide to Teaching Struggling Readers* (2004). We begin by sharing the key assumptions that underpin our orientation to working with struggling writers (see also Dudley-Marling and Paugh 2004).

Instructional Needs of Struggling Writers

It is usually assumed that struggling learners, particularly students with special needs, have "unique" instructional requirements—that is, deficits—that require specialized instruction. However, we do not believe this to be true of struggling writers, including remedial or special education students. There is no evidence that persuades us that struggling writers have *unique* instructional needs that require a form of writing instruction that is qualitatively different from the instruction provided to their more academically successful peers (Rhodes and Dudley-Marling 1996). Specifically, there isn't a pool of instructional interventions specific to struggling writers. On the contrary, differential instruction that denies struggling learners access to the same high-quality writing instruction provided to their more academically successful peers can have the effect of exacerbating learning problems (Dudley-Marling and Paugh 2005; Oakes 2005). Often this differential instruction takes the form of an *overemphasis* on the mechanics of writing (spelling, punctuation, and capitalization) at the expense of instruction in writing purposeful texts (Dyson and Freedman 2003; Graham, Harris, Fink-Chorzempa, and MacArthur 2003; Tomkins 2002).

Still, it is undeniable that many poor writers struggle with mechanics. Others have difficulty with planning and fluency (Graham, Harris, MacArthur, and Schwartz 1991). Struggling writers may also have difficulty anticipating the needs of their audience, "the constraints imposed by the topic, the development of rhetorical goals, [and] the organization of text" (Graham, Harris, and Larsen 2001, 75). Struggling writers frequently have trouble with word choice and revising their writing. Generally, they are less aware of the processes employed by more able writers (Graham, Harris, and Larsen 2001). None of these issues are unique to struggling writers, but they are much more likely than their peers to require writing instruction that is *frequent, intensive, explicit,* and *individualized* (Dudley-Marling and Paugh 2004). Illustrating what *frequent, intensive, explicit,* and *individualized* support and direction look like for struggling writers is the primary purpose of this book.

Organizing Instruction for Struggling Writers

Whole-class, one-size-fits-all approaches to writing instruction will never be congenial to the needs of individual, struggling writers, whose needs are widely varied. The key to meeting the instructional needs of struggling writers—in fact, of meeting the particular needs of even the most successful students—is individualized support and direction, informed by appropriate, ongoing assessment. To support struggling writers, teachers must be able to organize their classroom with structures that permit them to collect routine, in-depth assessment data and to work with students individually and in small groups.

Our preferred structure for organizing writing instruction is writing workshop (Atwell 1998; Calkins 1994; Fletcher and Portalupi 2001; Graves 1983). Writing workshop, with its emphasis on whole-class minilessons, independent writing time, and writing conferences, provides instructional spaces for teachers to assess the needs of individual students and provide *frequent, intensive, explicit,* and *individualized support and direction* as needed. As teachers work with students individually or in small groups, other students engage productively in purposeful writing, putting to use what they've learned about the craft of writing with the support of their teachers and peers. In the context of writing workshop, teachers push *all* students, including their least and most able students, as far as they can go as writers. Going as "far as they can" means learning to write effectively for a wide range of purposes and audiences.

It is important to emphasize the role of explicit support and direction in the context of the writing workshop. One of the most frequent criticisms of writing workshop is the assumption that, in the context of the workshop, "writing processes are self-learned" (Englert and Raphael 1988, 516), as if teachers just pass out the pencils and paper, stand back, and then wait for students to learn how to write well. This is a gross misrepresentation of the role of teachers in writing workshop. All students require some measure of explicit instruction tailored to their individual needs. Laissez-faire teaching is *never* good teaching. For struggling writers, explicit, individualized instructional support is crucial. However,

> explicit instruction need not imply a rigid, structuralist approach. Rather, it can entail a conscious attempt to focus students' attention on particular aspects of writing rather than expecting students to discover them on their own. The degree of explicit instruction we provide then is something with which each of us must struggle on an ongoing basis with every new group of students—indeed with each writing situation. (Chapman 1999, 488)

In other words, explicit instruction should not be equated with the mindless drill and practice of fragmented, decontextualized writing skills. Still, all students will require some measure of explicit teaching to help them learn the craft of writing effectively for particular audiences and purposes.

There Is Not *a* Writing Process

Closely linked to the structure of the writing workshop is a pedagogy that emphasizes the processes skilled writers use as they write for various purposes and audiences. This emphasis on process builds upon a significant body of research that has identified a range of practices skilled writers follow as they craft texts toward some purpose (e.g., personal communications, narrative and expository texts) and audience. These processes include selecting a topic, planning, rehearsing, accessing information, reading, organizing, editing, revising, considering the reader's point of view, attending to spelling and punctuation, and so on (Farnan and Dahl 2003; Englert and Raphael 1988). Struggling writers, almost by definition, have difficulty with one or more of these processes, such as planning or taking the perspective of intended audiences (Englert and Raphael 1988; Graham, Harris, MacArthur, and Schwartz 1991).

There have been serious misunderstandings about how theory and research on writing processes translate into writing instruction, however. In many of the elementary classrooms we have visited over the years, teachers had posted writing guidelines for their students (e.g., Brainstorm—Prewrite—Write—Revise—Publish) as if there is *a single, linear writing process* followed by all writers for all kinds of writing. Certainly, writers plan, write, edit, revise, and so on, but not in any fixed order; nor does every piece of writing require planning, editing, or revision. Moreover, the processes that writers use are a function of purpose, audience, and context (Dyson and Freedman 2003). Therefore, teachers of writing ought to focus their students' attention on processes used by effective writers, but not on a prescribed process. "Any classroom structures that demand that all students plan, write and revise on cue or in that order are likely to run into difficulty" (Dyson and Freedman 2003, 975).

The emphasis on process among teachers of writing has led some critics to question whether this focus has devalued the products of writing. For example, some critics suggest there is a long-term danger of making final drafts secondary to the process of drafting. We've all read articles in the newspaper criticizing teachers who, the writers claim, no longer care about spelling, punctuation, or grammar. Again, this is a misreading of writing process pedagogy. In reality, processes matter only insofar as they enable writers to fulfill their intentions, with particular audiences. Writing conventions matter precisely because they assist writers in fulfilling their intentions, but how these conventions work is a function of purpose, audience, and context. For example, how the conventions of grammar, spelling, and punctuation support writers' intentions is different in a formal essay than in an Instant Message (IM) or text message. In this book, we emphasize genre: writing content, forms, structures, and vocabulary appropriate for particular purposes, audiences, and social situations.

Goals for Writing Instruction

The overriding goal for writing instruction in elementary classrooms is *to push all students to write effectively for as wide a range of purposes and for as wide a range of audiences as possible.* The purposes for which people write include:

- Telling fictional stories (often with a secondary purpose of sharing some emotion, such as sadness or humor).
- Sharing experiences (e.g., journals, autobiographies).
- Recording and retelling events (diaries, biographies, historical records).
- Aiding memory (e.g., notes, lists, reminders).
- Writing research reports (and other academic forms of writing).
- Persuading (e.g., essays, editorials, advertising).
- Thinking and reflecting (e.g., notes to clarify their own thinking).
- Filling out forms.
- Labeling.
- Interacting or communicating with others (e.g., letters, notes, email, Instant Messaging).
- Giving directions (e.g., recipes, driving directions).
- Organizing (e.g., charts, PowerPoint presentations).
- Documenting learning (e.g., tests, including timed writing in response to prompts).
- Building and maintaining social relationships.

One additional purpose for writing that has become increasingly important is writing for testing situations, and teachers need to account for this purpose, too.

Purpose affects both the form and content of writing, but so does audience. Effective writers always write for an audience—even if the audience is oneself—and the audiences for whom people write vary according to their physical, temporal, and social distance. Writers may write to someone who is physically—or virtually—present (e.g., jotting a note to oneself, passing a note to a classmate, Instant Messaging) or geographically distant. They may write for an unknown audience or to people they know well. Writers may write to people with whom they share lots of background knowledge or to people relatively uninformed on the topic of their writing. Their writing may be read immediately (e.g., Instant Messaging) or weeks or years in the future (letters, books). All of these variables affect both the form and content of writing, reinforcing the advice that struggling readers must be chal-

A Classroom Teacher's Guide to Struggling Writers

lenged to write for a wide range of purposes (in and out of school) and audiences (not just the teacher).

The important point here is that writers don't learn to write "once and for all" (Gee 1996) as much as they learn to write *particular* texts for *particular* purposes and audiences. Writers' choices regarding style (formal vs. informal), vocabulary, grammar, content (degree of explicitness), form (poem vs. essay), and conventions such as spelling and punctuation are directly tied to purposes and audiences. The kind of text considered most appropriate for a high school English paper, for example, would be completely inappropriate for Instant Messaging (and visa versa). The challenge for young writers (and their teachers) is to learn how particular purposes—and audiences—give rise to particular textual, or genre, features (Chapman 1999). Again, this is why it is so important for teachers to challenge students to write and read as wide a range of genres as possible. An overemphasis on narrative texts, which is a common complaint about many writing workshops, denies students opportunities to learn how to use various textual features and conventions appropriate to write other kinds of texts. Similarly, students who learn only to write in response to writing prompts with imagined audiences learn only the genre of writing for timed tests and imaginary audiences.

To set goals for individual struggling writers, teachers must assess and determine how successfully students achieve their purposes in their writing. If a struggling writer produces unsuccessful pieces of writing (i.e., writing that fails to achieve its communicative purposes), the teacher asks, "What does this student need to learn to fulfill her intentions with her intended audience?" The ultimate evaluation of any piece of writing is this: Does it work? Writing skills matter, but only in the service of the writer's intentions. We'll have much more to say about this later.

Writing Is a Social Act

Writing is an inherently social activity. Writers always endeavor to achieve particular effects with particular audiences, even if that audience is oneself. Dyson (2001) puts it this way: "The process of becoming literate is an inherently social one; it entails learning to differentiate and manipulate the elements of the written system (e.g., letters and words) in order to engage with, and manipulate, the social world" (126).

Struggling students—indeed all students—must learn to write in genuinely social contexts. Students need to write routinely for *real* audiences (not just their teachers or hypothetical audiences) who will respond to the effectiveness of their writing—that is, who will determine whether it works to achieve the students' intentions. Students must have frequent opportunities to share their writing with other young writers who can offer feedback on the efficacy of their writing. Students also benefit from writing collaboratively—and playfully—with peers, which can increase attention to writing decisions (Dyson and Freedman 2003). Writing prospers when it is "a valued part of a social network, i.e., when it helps to mediate social relationships" (Dyson and Freedman 2003, 968). In Curt Dudley-Marling's third-grade class, for example, his students frequently wrote on topics that had the effect of building and maintaining relationships (Dudley-Marling 1997). The boys in his class, for example, often wrote adventure stories like "The Four Amigos" that featured characters named after friends or classmates they wanted to have as friends. In this context, writing becomes a natural part of the "social work" that goes on in any classroom (Dyson 1989, 1993).

The Importance of Student Voice

Students who have a personal investment in their writing are more likely to be motivated to learn and use the processes of skilled writing. Students are more likely to edit and revise their work, for example, if they have some control over the topics for which they write (Englert and Raphael 1988; Graves 1983). Don Graves (1994) put it this way: "When voice is strong, writing improves, along with the skills that help to improve writing" (81). Graves (1979) reported that young writers found it easier to revise when they wrote about their own experiences.

He argues, "Voice is the engine that sustains writers through the hard work of drafting and redrafting" (1994, 81–82).

The practice of assigned writing topics and story starters can have a detrimental effect on students' writing and their willingness to engage in the hard work of learning to write (Dudley-Marling and Oppenheimer 1995; Hansen 2003). Tom Newkirk (2002), for example, argues that topics that are often of interest to boys (e.g., popular culture) are often prohibited by teachers, which has an adverse effect on boys' enthusiasm for writing. In general, student writing flourishes when students exercise control over the topics, purposes, and audiences for their writing. As a group, struggling writers often have much less control over the form and content of their writing in school.

Of course, this does not mean that students need to exercise complete control over the content and form of their writing. The overriding goal of encouraging students to write a range of different kinds of texts means that teachers will sometimes push students away from certain topics (e.g., "What I did last weekend") to get them to work in different genres. It also seems reasonable for teachers to engage students periodically in genre studies in which there is an expectation that students will write for similar purposes and, perhaps, audiences. Still, there is no reason that teachers and students can't work together to identify topics of interest to students.

The reality of high-stakes tests, which frequently use assigned topics and story starters in timed writing formats, indicates a need to give students experience writing in these formats (Sudol and Sudol 1991). Although many educators see little value in this kind of writing, it would be grossly unfair not to help students learn how to succeed on high-stakes writing tests using these formats. Still, an overemphasis on preparing students to "write for the test" undermines the overarching goal of teaching students to write for a wide range of purposes and audiences. Teaching students to write for high-stakes testing formats does not prepare them for other kinds of writing.

Honoring students' voices, by allowing them to use writing to fulfill personal intentions, helps students discover the power of writing to make a difference in the world. For example, writing has the power to convey information, entertain, forge relationships, and influence how people think about the world in which they live. In this kind of instructional environment, students learn the skills of writing (i.e., genre features) for particular audiences across a range of social and academic purposes.

Finally, young writers' ability to find their voices is a function of their developing competence. Writers who are invested in their writing may be motivated to learn the skills of good writing, but learning the skills of writing will also have an effect on students' ability to take control of their writing. "Students who do not perceive themselves as being competent writers, who cannot successfully control the many cognitive and physical demands of most writing tasks, may be unwilling, or even unable, to take ownership of their writing tasks" (Spaulding 1989, 417).

The Reading-Writing Connection

Reading and writing are mutually reinforcing processes. Reading plays an important role in learning to write—and, no doubt, learning to write has a positive effect on reading development. Arguably, the principal source of data for young writers on spelling, punctuation, vocabulary, organization, and other genre conventions is reading (Smith 1981; Templeton 2003). The critical reading of texts in order to uncover an author's purpose(s), intended audience, and rhetorical strategies will, for example, prod students to consider the rhetoric of composition in their own writing. (For more on this subject and a discussion of the value of "Questioning the Author," see McKeown, Hamilton, Kucan, and Beck 1997.)

Similarly, students who are encouraged to generate their own spellings in the process of writing may simultaneously develop phonemic awareness and phonetic skills that have been linked to early reading development (Richgels 2001). Teachers who make reading-writing connections explicit strengthen the literacy development of all their students, especially their struggling writers. The reading-writing connection also suggests some level of integration of reading and writing instruction, a point we'll return to later.

A Classroom Teacher's Guide to Struggling Writers

The Need for Teachers of Writing to Write

Writing is hard work. Even the most accomplished writers sometimes find they have nothing to write about and struggle to find their voice. Skilled writers sometimes get stuck; they may decide to abandon a writing topic altogether. The processes they use also vary according to their purposes and audiences. For example, even the most skilled writers will not revise every piece of writing they produce. And different writers employ different processes. Some writers may painstakingly revise each sentence and paragraph as they write; other writers are satisfied to get their words down on paper, postponing revision until later.

Teachers who do not write themselves may have difficulty appreciating the struggles of novice writers. They may be more likely to insist on *a* writing process for all students, such as demanding that all writing be revised. Some may require students to complete every piece of writing they start. Furthermore, these teachers may be impatient with students who get stuck. It will always be difficult for anyone who does not write to be an effective teacher of writing. Teachers who write—and attend to their writing processes—are better able to anticipate the needs of novice and struggling writers.

This doesn't mean that teachers need to write for publication, only that they make an effort to write regularly, perhaps alongside their students during writing workshop. It is equally important for teachers to take the time to reflect on what they do in the process of writing. As writers knowledgeable about the writing process, teachers will have a much better sense of what they are aiming for as teachers of writing. They will also be able to share with their students their own writing processes as well as their struggles as writers. And they'll be able to illustrate how the demands of writing vary according to their purposes and audiences. On the other hand, as Frank Smith (1981) observed, teachers who dislike or fear writing "will demonstrate that writing is to be disliked or feared, just as a teacher who is only seen writing comments on children's work, reports for parents, or notes and exercises for classroom activities will demonstrate that writing is simply for administrative and classroom purposes" (240).

Summary

The teaching of writing is a principled process underpinned by sound theory, thoughtful research, and good pedagogy. The following list of principles summarizes what we have detailed in this chapter.

- The goal of writing instruction is not for students to learn a single process but a range of processes used by effective writers.

- Learning to write one genre is inadequate preparation for writing in other genres.

- Teachers must push all students, including struggling writers, to write effectively for as wide a range of purposes and for as wide a range of audiences as possible.

- Writing is most likely to flourish when students have some measure of control over the topics, purposes, and audiences for their writing.

- Struggling writers need the same high-quality writing instruction that is offered to the most able writers.

- Struggling writers are more likely than their peers to require writing instruction that is *frequent, intensive, explicit,* and *individualized.*

- An overemphasis on writing conventions often has the effect of exacerbating the problems of struggling writers.

- Reading is a crucial source of data for students about the features of effective writing.

- The fundamental question when assessing students' writing is: Does it work to fulfill the writer's intention(s) with the targeted audience?

- Teachers who write and reflect on their own writing processes will have a better sense of what they're aiming for as teachers of writing.

Portrait of a Workshop that Meets the Needs of Struggling Writers

Teachers who organize their classrooms around writing workshop create a structure that provides struggling writers with large blocks of time to write independently and/or to write collaboratively with their classmates (e.g., collaborative writing, peer editing). The writing workshop also provides a structure for teachers to work with struggling students individually and in small groups, and to collect the routine assessment data needed to provide struggling writers with instruction appropriate to their individual needs. In general, the structure of writing workshop makes it possible for teachers to create welcoming, inclusive classrooms that are responsive to the wide range of experiences, abilities, and cultural and linguistic backgrounds students bring with them to school.

In this chapter, we present vignettes from Mrs. Mitchell's fourth-grade classroom to illustrate elements of writing workshop and the potential of a workshop format to support struggling writers.

An Environment that Supports Writing

Writing workshop was a defining feature of Mrs. Mitchell's fourth-grade classroom. Each day she set aside sixty minutes for writing instruction, which followed a ninety-minute reading block that was also organized around a workshop format (see Dudley-Marling and Paugh 2004). The boundaries between the reading and writing blocks in Mrs. Mitchell's classroom were permeable, however, in accordance with her belief that there must be a close relationship between reading and writing instruction. We observed a struggling writer named Sarah, for example, who was uncertain of the conventions for presenting dialogue in a piece she was writing. Mrs. Mitchell pointed her to several picture books that made extensive use of dialogue, and as a result, Sarah spent much of her writing time looking through the books. In this way, reading was directly related to writing. Mrs. Mitchell later followed up with a brief writing conference to talk with Sarah about what she had learned about the use of quotation marks from the books she had skimmed.

We observed other instances of overlap between reading and writing workshops during our visits to Mrs. Mitchell's classroom. For instance, Mrs. Mitchell often challenged her struggling writers and readers with word study activities during both workshops to support their development of spelling and phonics skills. It was also common for Mrs. Mitchell to refer her students to books to learn something about the writer's craft, as she did for Sarah. And Mrs. Mitchell often conducted minilessons that connected to both reading and writing (see the section that follows). In general, the boundaries between reading and writing workshops in Mrs. Mitchell's classroom were blurred.

Mrs. Mitchell organized the physical spaces in her classroom strategically to encourage and support her students' writing. Round tables—rather than desks—provided comfortable places for students to write together, if they wished. Mrs. Mitchell was aware that research indicates that, if given the opportunities, students often use writing to build and maintain social relationships (Dudley-Marling 1997; Dyson 1993). Her experience also told her that the immediate social possibilities of writing often motivate struggling and reluctant writers. As Anne Dyson (2001) puts it, "The process of becoming literate

A Classroom Teacher's Guide to Struggling Writers

is an inherently social one; it entails learning to differentiate and manipulate the elements of the written system (e.g., letters and words) in order to engage with, and manipulate, the social world" (126).

It was common for students in Mrs. Mitchell's fourth grade to situate their writing in social worlds. They often wrote collaborative stories, frequently shared their writing with classmates, and routinely helped edit each other's writing. They also used writing to celebrate and solidify friendships. On one particular day, R.J., Grant, Tony, and Ian, a struggling writer, illustrated a story about stunt riders, featuring themselves as the lead characters (see Figure 2.1). The boys spent more than a week writing this six-page story, which a classroom volunteer eventually typed for them.

In a bid to be included in this group, George wrote his own adventure story that featured himself, Tony, Grant, R.J., and Ian. On the same day, Andrea and Linda coauthored a story that included them both as characters lost in a haunted house. Shirin and Melissa,

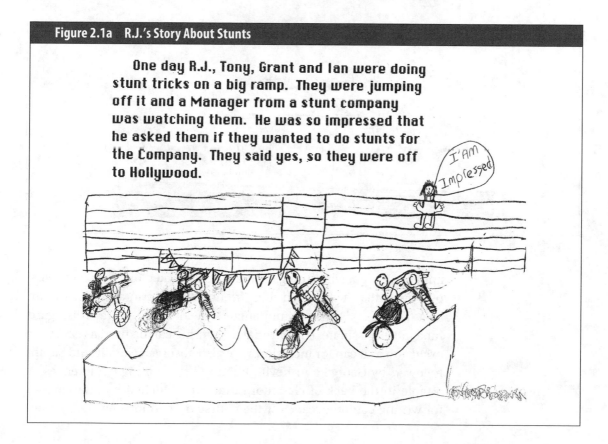

Figure 2.1a   R.J.'s Story About Stunts

One day R.J., Tony, Grant and Ian were doing stunt tricks on a big ramp. They were jumping off it and a Manager from a stunt company was watching them. He was so impressed that he asked them if they wanted to do stunts for the Company. They said yes, so they were off to Hollywood.

Portrait of a Workshop that Meets the Needs of Struggling Writers

Figure 2.1b

When they got there, they made arrangements for bikes and the hotel rooms. Then they went to the track where they would be doing their stunts. They got to see their new bikes. Tony's number was 5, Grant's number was 16, Ian's number was 200, and R.J.'s number was 21. They always did their stunts in pairs. That night there were 100's and 100's of people, so they got their costumes on, and they were so good that all the other shows there were even more people than before. Their fans loved them so much that they elected them for the Bikers' Of The Year award. They got to do their stunts all around the world.

another student who struggled as a writer, worked together on a piece of writing that highlighted their friendship ("Shirin and Melissa are best friends . . .") while simultaneously expressing mutual disregard for a male classmate. (Unfortunately, writing can be used as easily for exclusion as it can for inclusion.) We also observed Natalie and Sarah, followed by George and Kevin, holding brief editing conferences at a table in the back of classroom that Mrs. Mitchell had designated for writing conferences. Over the course of the morning, Sean, Jane, and Mark shared their writing with friends, and several other students briefly consulted with classmates on spelling. Throughout the year, it was common for Mrs. Mitchell's students to collaborate on pieces of writing, an arrangement that proved particularly beneficial to her struggling writers.

Following her belief that writing materials influence the kind of writing students do—as well as their inclination to write—Mrs. Mitchell provided her students with a range of writing materials and writing implements that were easy to access from a cabinet in the middle of her classroom. There, her students could find a variety of writing materials, including:

- Lined and unlined 8½″ × 11″ paper.
- Various sizes of unlined newsprint and construction paper.
- Recycled paper (cut in half).
- Card stock.
- Stationery.
- Long strips of tagboard.
- Index cards.
- Chart paper.
- Notepads.
- Sticky notes.

Each of these materials invited a different kind of writing. Unlined newsprint, for example, encouraged students to draw pictures and write shorter texts. Stationery encouraged letter writing. Strips of tagboard were useful for creating labels. Lined paper invited students to write longer texts, such as stories. Half sheets of recycled paper were convenient for writing notes to friends. Notepads encouraged students to take notes at the science center. And so on.

In addition to the materials in the cabinet, two computers near the blackboard in the front of the room offered students opportunities to participate in a range of engagements with print, including email and Instant Messaging (which Mrs. Mitchell used to introduce students to the concept of *genre*). Because Mrs. Mitchell found that various writing tools fostered different sorts of writing engagements, she also made available an old typewriter, pencils, pens, colored pencils, crayons, and chalk for students to write or draw with. Overall, Mrs.

Mitchell discovered that a wide range of writing implements and materials was particularly motivating to students who had previously been reluctant to write.

A fundamental goal for Mrs. Mitchell was to push all of her students to produce as many different kinds of writing (i.e., genres) as possible. In other words, she wanted her students to write for a wide range of purposes and audiences. Over the years, Mrs. Mitchell had learned that expanding the range of genres that her students wrote increased the chances that her struggling writers would discover a kind of writing that engaged them. One way she addressed this goal was by immersing her students in a wide range of print genres. The walls of her classroom were covered with lists, signs, directions, jokes, comic strips, poetry, song lyrics, newspaper articles, student writing, and so on. Comic books, magazines, newspapers, encyclopedias, advertising fliers, and a variety of Internet resources invited reading while modeling different kinds of writing for Mrs. Mitchell's students. Differently formatted books—big books, pop-up books, peekaboo books, accordion books, touch-and-feel books, picture books, chapter books, wordless picture books, and multimedia (e.g., Web-enhanced) texts—engaged the interest of many struggling readers and writers in Mrs. Mitchell's class and suggested different writing projects for students to try.

Writing Minilessons

Early in the school year, based on her routine assessment of students' writing, Mrs. Mitchell noticed a problem common among her fourth-grade students. She observed that many of her students were producing a generic style of writing that made few accommodations to the particular needs of readers. Although this was a general problem among her students—which she partly attributed to the third-grade teacher's emphasis on writing to prompts—it was particularly acute among the struggling writers in her class (see Tompkins 2002). George, for example, had been writing letters during writing workshop, but he used the same informal, colloquial style whether he was writing notes to his friends or fan letters to his favorite movie stars.

Melissa, who was writing a Big Book she hoped would be read by first graders, was having difficulty producing language appropriate for an audience of six- and seven-year-olds. Carl, another student who found writing difficult, was writing a memoir, but his writing offered a scanty level of detail appropriate only to readers who already knew him well. Michael often wrote stories that amused the boys, but his writing offended many of the girls. Based on these observations, Mrs. Mitchell planned a series of extended, whole-class minilessons designed to heighten her students' awareness of audience.

The first in this series of minilessons drew on a recent experience shared by most of Mrs. Mitchell's students. It had been cool and rainy during the first few weeks of September, and Mrs. Mitchell's students had been complaining about a school rule that prohibited children from entering the building before 8:00 A.M.—even though some of the buses arrived as early as 7:45 A.M. Mrs. Mitchell began the mini-lesson by proposing that, with her help, students write letters to Ms. Kaplansky, the principal, to persuade her to allow students into the school building earlier on rainy days. Mrs. Mitchell's fourth graders readily agreed, and a lively discussion about how to convince Ms. Kaplansky to revise her policy followed. When one of the students suggested that, because Ms. Kaplansky was the principal, the letters needed to be very polite, Mrs. Mitchell agreed that persuasive letters needed to consider the principal's status. She then suggested they make a list of what they knew about Ms. Kaplansky. Here's the list Mrs. Mitchell's students generated:

- This is her first year as principal.
- She's nice to the children.
- She's trying to learn children's names.
- Her first name is Margaret.
- She doesn't like noise in the hallways.
- She's younger than Mr. Wheeler [the previous principal].
- She doesn't have her own children.

Mrs. Mitchell then asked her students to consider the points they should make in their letters if they hoped to convince the principal to change her policy. Kevin suggested they tell her that the children on the early bus sometimes had to wait outside in the rain for nearly fifteen minutes, so even with raincoats and umbrellas their shoes got soaked. Sharon said that her hair got wet one day and she was cold all morning. Marla offered that they would have to convince Ms. Kaplansky that, if they were let into the school before 8:00 A.M., they would promise to behave.

Once they had agreed on the main points they wanted to cover in their letters, Mrs. Mitchell asked one more question: How would they address the principal in their letters? Should they call her *Margaret*? *Mrs. Kaplansky*? Or something else? Students agreed that *Dear Margaret* would be rude, since most grown-ups consider it impolite to call adults by their first names. Rashida suggested that the principal might not even read the letters if she thought students weren't being respectful. Students also rejected the suggestion that the letters begin *Dear Principal*, which most students thought was too impersonal. Everyone agreed that *Dear Ms. Kaplansky* was best. Kevin volunteered that it would be important to double-check spelling in their letters. When Mrs. Mitchell asked her class why this was so important, another student answered, "If there are lots of spelling mistakes, Ms. Kaplansky will think we didn't really care." Mrs. Mitchell agreed and then sent her students off to write their own letters.

To build on these points, Mrs. Mitchell conducted several other minilessons throughout the year to heighten students' awareness of the importance of considering the needs of the audience in their writing. She also followed up on these minilessons in individual writing conferences by asking students to think about whom they were writing for and how the audience for their writing might affect the form and content of their writing.

This lesson highlighted an issue that is central to writing instruction: To be effective, writers must learn to adjust the form and content of their writing to the needs of their audience. This is a particular problem for many struggling writers who, like George in the previous example, may not adapt the form of their writing according their purposes and the needs of their audience. Not all teachers will have an occasion to have their students write to the principal, but all students will benefit from opportunities to write for authentic audiences.

Several weeks later we observed a different kind of minilesson in Mrs. Mitchell's classroom. This one connected with a minilesson she had presented at the opening of the reading workshop. Together, these minilessons were designed to highlight decisions writers make in the process of writing, something not apparent to many developing writers. Here's what took place.

Mrs. Mitchell began the reading minilesson by reading her students the introduction to "Cedric," a story by Tove Jansson (1995). The story begins with the following text:

> This story takes place in Moominvalley, an imaginary land inhabited by many unusual creatures, such as hemulens and fillyjonks. Living there, too, are the Moominfamily—Moominpappa, Moominmamma, and Moomintroll—and their companions, Sniff and Snufkin. (150)

After reading the introduction, Mrs. Mitchell asked her class, "Why do you think the author tells us this at the very beginning of the story?" Marla suggested the author "wanted us to know the names of the characters." Kevin offered that "maybe she told us that Moominvalley was in an 'imaginary land' so we'd know this was fiction." After a bit more discussion, Mrs. Mitchell read the rest of the story to her students. She then turned her students' attention back to the introduction and asked, "Now that you've heard the whole story, is there anything else you think the author should have told us in the beginning?" Sarah commented that there were "quite a few words in the story I didn't know. Maybe the author could have told us what these words meant before the story." Several students disagreed. Carl, for example, suggested, "If you don't know some of the words you can look them up in the dictionary." This discussion lasted for several more minutes. The purpose of this reading minilesson was to help students think about how authors sometimes use introductions to help readers understand what follows (Beck, McKeown, Hamilton, and Kucan 1997).

The same day, Mrs. Mitchell conducted a writing minilesson in which she presented the introduction from a piece of writing produced by Rashida—with Rashida's permission. Rashida had written a story about several adventures involving her and her two best friends, a story that had been read by most of Rashida's classmates. Rashida began her story by briefly telling her readers a little bit about herself and her friends, Natalie and Sarah: how long they had been friends, where they lived, what they liked to do, and so on. Mrs. Mitchell asked the same questions she had asked in her reading lesson: "Why do you think Rashida told us this now?" Then she asked the class to read Rashida's story. After they finished reading, she asked: "Is there anything else she could have told her readers to help them read her story?" Mrs. Mitchell wanted her students to think about how introductions could be used to set up what followed in their own writing. This minilesson reinforced other minilessons Mrs. Mitchell had conducted to help students focus on their readers' needs as they wrote and revised their writing.

Lessons like these highlight writers' decision-making processes as they write for particular purposes and audiences. Additionally, these lessons point children to perhaps the most important source for learning how to write effectively: authors. If we want students to learn about writing introductions, adding details, creating dialogue, using punctuation, or working with various genres, we cannot do better than to point our students to authors who do these things well—and that often includes student authors.

Independent Writing Time

Through the use of minilessons that focused on writing, Mrs. Mitchell was able to address common writing problems and introduce new ideas to her students. But most of the work of her writing workshop was accomplished during the forty to fifty minutes Mrs. Mitchell set aside each day for independent writing. Extended blocks of writing time gave Mrs. Mitchell's students opportunities for sustained engagement in writing—a chance to practice skills they had learned previously in minilessons and during writing conferences. And while students were working independently, Mrs. Mitchell was able to take the time to conduct careful, ongoing assessment of their writing. These assessments, conducted in the context of routine writing conferences, informed the intensive, explicit, individual support and direction she offered students during her writing conferences.

Sean, for example, was a reluctant writer who hadn't written anything for days because he'd been having trouble finding a topic. When Mrs. Mitchell conferenced with Sean on this particular day, he was still struggling to think of a topic he wanted to write about. Mrs. Mitchell began by asking Sean to talk about how he liked to spend his time out of school.

Mrs. Mitchell: So, Sean, I see you're still having some trouble thinking of a topic to write about.

Sean: Yeah. I just can't think of anything anyone would want to read about.

Mrs. Mitchell: Did you make a list of possible topics like I suggested?

Sean: Uh, huh. But then I shared the list with Carl, and he didn't think any of them were interesting.

Mrs. Mitchell: Well, Carl is hard to please. Why don't you share your list of topics with me?

Sean: All right. [*Pause while he locates the list in his writing folder*] Here's the list: Another story about the adventures of Sean and Corwin; a story about a man who can fly; a story about a talking dog; a mystery about a famous detective named Sean; and a mystery called "the disappearing principal." What do you think?

Mrs. Mitchell: I think there are several interesting topics here. Do you feel passionately about any of them?

Sean: Not really.

Mrs. Mitchell: OK, then. Maybe this will help. All these topics are fiction and, if I remember correctly, you've written mostly fiction this year. Is that right?

Sean: Yeah.

Mrs. Mitchell: So here's an idea. Maybe it's time to move on to another genre. You might enjoy writing some nonfiction like we talked about in one of our minilessons last week.

Sean: I tried to think of a nonfiction piece last week but I couldn't think of anything I could write about.

Mrs. Mitchell: I seem to remember that you and your dad like to fly kites in the park. Is that right?

Sean: Kite flying is awesome.

Mrs. Mitchell: Well, maybe you could write a little how-to book on flying kites. It's something you know a lot about, and I'm sure the other kids would be interested.

Sean: Mmm.

Mrs. Mitchell: I think you might start by looking at some of the how-to books we have in our classroom library to see how other authors put these kind of books together. Just a second, Sean. [*She leaves for a minute and comes back with three how-to books for children: one about making paper airplanes; one about painting on rocks; and one making pop-ups.*] Here are a few books you might find helpful. Pay special attention to how these authors go about giving their audiences directions, how they organize their texts, and how they use illustrations [Schleppegrell and Go 2007]. Take a look and we'll talk again tomorrow.

Mrs. Mitchell's conference with Sean illustrates several of the principles we discussed in Chapter 1. First, Mrs. Mitchell pushed Sean to try out a new genre, moving beyond the fiction that had dominated his writing. Additionally, she found a way to build on Sean's interest in kite flying even as she encouraged him to try out a new kind of writing (nonfiction). Mrs. Mitchell also drew on the work of published authors to help Sean learn about the procedural language important to structuring how-to books. And she did all this in a context that allowed her to focus on Sean's individual needs as a writer.

When she finished her conference with Sean, Mrs. Mitchell gathered a small group of students who were ready to learn how to use dialogue in their writing. This group included Lloyd, who had a difficult time figuring out how to use punctuation in his writing.

Mrs. Mitchell also met individually with Sarah, whom she had asked to look through several books to see what she could learn about how commercial writers use dialogue. After a quick discussion about how dialogue helps brings characters' thoughts and feelings to life, Mrs. Mitchell asked Sarah to share what she learned with several other classmates who were working on narratives of their own.

Mrs. Mitchell then conducted several quick check-in conferences with Andrea and Linda, Melissa and Shirin, and the other students who were writing collaborative pieces, to keep track of how these pieces were progressing and to offer help if students were having problems. For example, she began her check-in conference with Melissa and Shirin by simply asking, "How's the writing going?" Melissa answered, "OK," and Mrs. Mitchell asked her to read what they had written so far. When Melissa finished reading, Mrs. Mitchell asked if they needed any help from her. They said they didn't, so Mrs. Mitchell made a few notes:

- Shirin and Melissa continue with "friendship" piece.
- Will need help editing their piece for spelling.
- Among a number of students who would benefit from minilessons on increasing variety of word choice.
- Next time ask them about how they'd like to share their writing.

It is essential for teachers to document their observations of students. Carefully documented writing conferences and observations of students' writing provide the detailed assessment data teachers require to provide struggling learners—indeed all learners—with writing instruction appropriate to their needs.

After she completed her check-in conferences Mrs. Mitchell met with Erica, a new student in her class. Mrs. Mitchell first asked Erica to talk about her writing. (She was writing about how she missed her friends at her old school.) She then asked Erica a series of questions she hoped would give her a sense of how Erica saw herself as a writer.

Mrs. Mitchell: Erica, do you think you're a good writer?

Erica: I guess so. We wrote every day in my old school. I like to write, but sometimes I can't think of much to write about.

Mrs. Mitchell: Anything else?

Erica: I'm not a very good speller.

Mrs. Mitchell: What do you think you need to learn to be a better writer?

Erica: I need more good ideas to write about.

Mrs. Mitchell: Anything else?

Erica: Spelling. I want to learn to spell more words.

Mrs. Mitchell: OK. What can I do to help you?

Erica: I don't know. Maybe you could help me learn to use more words in my writing.

Mrs. Mitchell: Thanks, Erica.

Mrs. Mitchell made some notes about her conversation with Erica and moved on to meet individually with Kevin and Michael, two students who had requested writing conferences. Kevin shared a memoir-style piece he'd been writing the last few days, after Mrs. Mitchell had conducted several minilessons on memoir. Kevin was trying to write about the birth of his baby sister, but he was having some difficulty deciding exactly what he should say. He questioned how much detail he should provide about himself. This prompted a discussion about his intended audience and what, if anything, they already knew or needed to know about him.

Michael, on the other hand, simply wanted Mrs. Mitchell to read his piece and tell him if she thought it was ready for editing. She agreed that it was.

At this point, Mrs. Mitchell ended the independent writing period by calling her students to the carpet to share their writing briefly with the whole group.

Sharing

The last five to ten minutes of Mrs. Mitchell's writing workshop provided an opportunity for students to share and discuss their writing. Some days she just asked students to share their topics as a way of modeling different writing ideas for her students. This benefited students who had difficulty coming up with topics, as well as students whom Mrs. Mitchell was pushing to try new genres. Other days she asked students if they had encountered—or solved—any problems with their writing. These discussions were aimed at students who needed a more realistic sense of the hard work associated with writing effective texts. Occasionally, she'd spend this brief period merely commenting on what she'd observed during independent writing time.

It is important to point out that Mrs. Mitchell spent a considerable amount of time early in the school year modeling and discussing appropriate ways for students to respond to each other's writing by focusing on the writer's intention and audience. On this particular day, R.J., Grant, Tony, and Ian offered to share a draft of their ongoing adventure story (see Figure 2.1). When they finished reading their text, Mrs. Mitchell invited questions or comments from the rest of the class. Mark asked the boys where they had gotten the idea for their story. Sarah wanted to know what they'd be doing with their story after it was edited. Kevin asked if they planned on writing any more stories about the "four amigos."

A Classroom Teacher's Guide to Struggling Writers

Kevin then shared his still-in-progress piece about this baby sister. Erica asked if Kevin was writing about himself or someone else. This led Mrs. Mitchell to ask Kevin to think about their earlier conversation about audience if he made additional revisions to his piece.

Sample Lesson Plan

This section includes an example of Mrs. Mitchell's lesson plan for the day described in this chapter (see Figure 2.2). Note that her plan focuses on the *instructional needs of individual students*, recognizing that whole-class instructional planning rarely considers the needs of struggling learners.

Figure 2.2   Sample Lesson Plan

Lesson Plan: Wednesday, November 16
10:30–11:30 **Writing Instruction**
    Writing Minilesson (10:30–10:40)
    Goal: Draw students' attention to how writers sometimes use introductions to give needed background information to readers. Follows up on reading minilesson and other lessons on needs of readers

- Recall reading minilesson earlier in the day, using the excerpt from "Cedric." Emphasize how Jansson uses introduction to introduce readers to characters and setting.

- Use overhead to show introduction to Rashida's piece, which describes her and her friends.

- Briefly describe Rashida's piece. Then ask, "Why do you think Rashida decided to tell us about herself and her friends at the beginning of her piece?"

- Have students read her piece.

- Then ask: "Do you think there is anything else she could have included in her introduction that would be helpful to her readers?"

Figure 2.2 *(continued)*

- Remind students how they must always be thinking about both their purpose and their audience.

Independent Writing

- Sean's stuck. Help with writing topic. Push to try some nonfiction (maybe related to kite flying).

- Quick check-in conferences with kids who are writing collaboratively: Andrea and Linda; Melissa and Shirin; R.J., Grant, Tony, and Ian.

- Do quick self-assessment with Erica.

- Sarah: Use of dialogue. Point her to several texts using dialogue for her to look at and consider.

- Sarah, Caitlin, Tamim: Use of dialogue in their writing. Have Sarah share what she learned.

- See who requested individual conferences.

11:25 **Sharing**
Today, see if anyone wants to share their writing.

Summary

These brief vignettes offer a glimpse into writing workshop in one fourth-grade classroom that was organized to support the needs of individual students regardless of their writing ability. The struggling writers required more frequent, intensive, and explicit support and direction from Mrs. Mitchell, but all of her students benefited from a structure that allowed her to provide individualized attention that focused on her students' particular needs. To take full advantage of the potential of a writing workshop format, Mrs. Mitchell made sure to create her minilessons and focus her writing conferences directly in response to students' individual needs. Her clear instructional goals, her well-planned instruction (which she based on her ongoing assessment of students' needs), and her routine reflection on students' learning enabled her to use writing workshop to address the learning needs of each student in her classroom, including the needs of the struggling writers.

3

Writing Workshop

Minilessons

A writing workshop is an effective way to organize classroom time and space in a manner that supports the needs of struggling writers. As the vignettes in Chapter 2 illustrate, the structure of writing workshop creates time and space for teachers to provide the frequent, intensive, explicit, and individualized support and direction that is fundamental to the growth of struggling writers. However, the benefits of writing workshop are not limited to struggling writers: The flexibility of writing workshop enables teachers to address the needs of even the most proficient writers. The structure of writing workshop also offers students extended blocks of time to write on a routine basis, which is particularly important. Effective writing instruction demands a regular, predictable schedule that gives all students, particularly struggling writers, extended periods of time for scaffolded writing instruction each day. Don Graves (1994) argues that "if students are not engaged in writing at least four days out of five, and for a period of thirty-five to forty minutes, beginning in first grade, they will have little opportunity to learn to think through the medium of writing" (104).

A predictable writing schedule supports another goal of writing instruction: giving students opportunities to shape a single piece of writing over a period of days (or even weeks). The all-too-common practice of writing a new piece every writing period, with or without writing prompts, prepares students only for the kind of "throw-away" writing that is rare outside of school settings. Sticking with a piece of writing enables developing writers to learn the writer's craft by experiencing the hard work of shaping a piece of writing over time. Effective writing instruction for struggling writers isn't about writing more, but writing better (with the support of teachers); specifically, learning the skills associated with specific writing genres.

Two of the most important structural features of the writing workshop are minilessons and independent writing time. We explore minilessons in this chapter and discuss independent writing time in Chapter 4.

Minilessons: An Overview

Minilessons are a structural feature of most writing workshops. Many teachers begin their writing workshops with brief, whole-class minilessons, but we also know teachers who prefer to conduct minilessons at the end of the writing workshop, after students have engaged in a period of independent writing. In either case, minilessons offer teachers opportunities to address writing issues relevant to most students in the class, including students for whom writing is difficult. This is a time when teachers can introduce a new writing genre, teach a skill, model a strategy, discuss organizational issues or problems, invite students to brainstorm possible writing topics, and so on.

Minilessons are typically short, lasting five to ten minutes, although, occasionally, longer minilessons can be useful. Keeping minilessons brief and focused aligns with the principle of not teaching students what they already know or what they are not ready to learn, a problem with many whole-class lessons. For instance, lengthy whole-class lessons on particular forms of punctuation, such as quotation marks, will be an inefficient use of writing time for students who aren't yet ready to use them or who already have control of these skills. However, teachers can often draw on the expertise of more able writers during minilessons. During a lesson on quotation marks, for example, students who already have a strong sense of the conventions can share with classmates their sense of how and when they use quotation marks in their writing. Meanwhile, students who aren't using dialogue in their writing—and, therefore, may not be ready to learn about quotation marks—can still benefit from this minilesson because it introduces something for them to consider in their future writing. Of course, to help students make these connections, teachers should follow up brief minilessons with individual conferences or small-group work.

The planning of minilessons is informed by teachers' ongoing assessment of their students and by state, provincial, and local language arts frameworks. A second-grade teacher who notices that many of her students are uncertain about the use of periods in their writing might design a series of minilessons to address this issue. A third-grade teacher in Massachusetts might use minilessons to talk about "writing stories containing details of the setting," since this is a standard specified by the *Massachusetts English Language Arts Curriculum Framework* (Massachusetts Department of Education 2001).

In the rest of this chapter, we present three types of minilessons (adapted from Hindley 1998):

- Minilessons that address management and organizational issues.
- Minilessons that focus on writing skills and strategies.
- Minilessons that address the qualities of good writing.

In Chapter 5, we will also discuss minilessons that examine specific language features associated with various writing genres, including the formal, academic writing genres that are highly valued in school.

Minilessons that Address Management and Organizational Issues

We know many teachers who have been reluctant to implement a workshop approach with struggling learners because they worry that writing workshops lack the structure that struggling learners need. The reality is that writing workshops are carefully structured by clearly articulated goals, predictable routines, explicit standards of behavior, and well-organized spaces.

A Classroom Teacher's Guide to Struggling Writers

Many teachers use minilessons to teach their students the routines of the writing workshop. When Curt Dudley-Marling taught third grade, for example, he used a whole-class minilesson to give his students a tour of the classroom to learn how the writing workshop was arranged. For instance, on the tour they briefly discussed the cabinet where students could find writing materials; the table at the back of the room where students could write quietly; the spaces where students could share and discuss their writing; the publishing center near the front of the room; the computer center; and so on. He also used minilessons to help students create some rules of conduct for writing workshop. He displayed the "Rules for Writing Workshop" poster in a prominent spot at the rear of the classroom, and when some students had difficulty settling down during independent writing time, he eventually added his own rule to the list: "No talking during the first five minutes of independent writing time" (see Figure 3.1).

Occasionally, he gathered his students together during independent writing time to remind them of the rules of conduct for writing workshop, particularly early in the school year. But, as the year progressed, students learned to work well within these routines, and

---

Figure 3.1   Rules for Writing Workshop

1. You must be writing, talking about writing, or consulting a writing resource.

2. Talking is OK, but don't disturb other students.

3. Don't interrupt Mr. Dudley-Marling when he's conferencing with another student.

4. If you need help, use the "conference sign up sheet."

5. Use the sign up sheet if you want to use the computer for writing.

6. You can write anywhere in the classroom, but use the "Quiet" table if you don't want to be disturbed.

7. No talking during the first five minutes of independent writing time.

management issues seldom arose. In general, students welcome opportunities to write for purposes and audiences of interest to them. In our experience, classroom management is not usually much of an issue during independent writing time, provided that teachers have carefully introduced students to the structures and expectations of a writing workshop.

Minilessons that Focus on Writing Skills and Strategies

Minilessons are an effective way to help struggling writers learn about the range of skills and strategies writers use in the process of planning, composing, revising, and editing texts, and about how these processes vary according to the writers' purposes and audiences. Writing minilessons can be used, for example, to:

- Brainstorm writing topics.
- Teach writing conventions, such as spelling and punctuation.
- Share techniques for organizing or planning writing, such as using graphic organizers.
- Illustrate decision making in the process of writing.
- Teach revision and proofreading.

In this section we describe various minilesson formats that teachers can adapt to teach the skills and strategies writers use in the process of composing and revising texts. To help struggling writers, teachers may need to follow up on these whole-class minilessons in individual writing conferences and small-group lessons.

Modeling Writing Processes

Frank Smith (1981) observed that "writing is often hard work; it requires concentration, physical effort, and a tolerance for frustration and disappointment" (238). Many struggling writers do not seem to understand that writing is often difficult—and sometimes frustrating—for all writers. They may not know that even the best writers sometimes get stuck, perhaps giving up on some texts entirely. Many struggling writers are surprised to learn that good writers don't always produce their best writing. Donald Graves (1983) reported that students' best writing is often followed by several less successful writing efforts. Purposes, audiences, and topics all affect writers' engagement with particular texts. And sometimes good writers just have off days. All of this information will surprise many struggling writers.

To help struggling writers become aware of the hard work of writing, teachers can model their own writing processes during minilessons. Mrs. Travers, a third-grade teacher, sometimes composes stories on an overhead transparency during minilessons, talking out loud as she writes in order to give her students some sense of a writer's moment-to-moment decision making during the writing process. For example, one day during writing workshop, she approached the overhead projector and began the minilesson like this:

> I was thinking that I might write about something that happened last night when my husband and I were walking our dog. We saw a fox pup when were walking along a trail toward Fawn Lake. It was very exciting. So I have a topic but, before I do any writing, I need to decide whom I should write for. I also need to decide what kind of writing I'd like to do.
>
> My mother would be interested, so I could write her a letter or an email. Or I could write a story for Ms. Wheeler's kindergarteners.
>
> My husband got some good pictures of the fox pup. It might make a nice picture book. My local newspaper likes to publish little nature articles by people in the community, so I could write something for the paper. Hmm. Well, I think I'd like to try writing a picture book to share with Ms. Wheeler's class.
>
> How should I start?

Mrs. Travers began to write on the overhead transparency, reading the words aloud.

> *Mary, Tim, and Moxy are getting ready for a walk.* No, that's not very interesting.

She crossed out this sentence.

> Kindergarteners would be more interested if I focused on our dog, Moxy.

She started writing again.

> *Moxy is a Labrador Retriever. She loves chasing the cat. She loves fetching tennis balls. She likes sleeping in the sun.*

Mrs. Travers stopped to replace *she* with *Moxy* in each sentence. Then she resumed writing.

> *Moxy's favorite thing to do is taking walks. . . .*

Mrs. Travers continued to write for a few more minutes.

> I'm going to finish this story at home. To make this into a picture book, I'm also going to have to decide how much text to write on each page and decide where to put pictures.

Several days later, Mrs. Travers shared a draft of the story of "Moxy and the Baby Fox" with her class.

Mrs. Travers' choice to write about an everyday experience in this minilesson was deliberate. Earlier in the year, she had shared a piece of writing about a trip to France, hoping this would invite students to write about their own trips. Most students had embraced this chance, but after independent writing time, a boy named Troy shared that he had not done any writing. The problem? He'd "never traveled to any exciting places like France." From that moment, Mrs. Travers resolved to write only about everyday experiences her students were likely to share.

Several weeks later, Mrs. Travers focused another minilesson on "Moxy and the Baby Fox" to model revision strategies. Mrs. Travers talked out loud while she revised her story:

> Deleting: "I don't think I need this sentence since I've already talked about where we found the fox pup."

> Moving text: "It might make more sense to talk about Moxy sleeping in the sun before I talk about what she likes to chase."

> Inserting text: "Oops. It isn't clear how my dog could have gotten so far off the trail. I need to say something about letting her off the leash here."

> Substituting words: "I've already called the fox *tiny* twice. I need another word here. Maybe I could call it *diminutive*. No, that's too hard a word for kindergarteners. Maybe I could just refer to its length, or say *it's no longer than my hand*."

As she revised, Mrs. Travers also modeled the use of various revision tools, such as including arrows to indicate the moving of text, drawing lines through words to delete them, using carets to insert text, and so on.

On another occasion, Mrs. Travers used an email to a manufacturer about a defective product to illustrate how her choice of wording was affected by her purpose (getting a refund) and her audience (a customer service representative about whom she knew nothing). Over the course of the academic year, Mrs. Travers used minilessons to model these processes:

- Brainstorming writing topics.
- Overcoming writer's block.
- Responding to other people's writing.
- Spelling unknown words.
- Noticing unusual spellings in the process of reading, proofreading, and editing.

She also provided more minilessons on revision, a particular focus for most of her struggling writers.

Modeling is a powerful strategy for opening a window into the decision making that stands behind the writing process. It is particularly important to teachers to offer struggling writers a clear look at the intellectual work involved in the writing process, because they are often unaware of what effective writers think about in the process of composing and revising texts.

Demonstrating Writing Strategies

Minilessons offer opportunities for teachers to provide whole-class demonstrations of various strategies effective writers use prior to or during the process of composing texts. For example, Ms. Krauss, a second-grade teacher, wanted to demonstrate the value of talk as a strategy that writers use when they get stuck, so she invited another teacher, Mrs. Collins, to collaborate on a minilesson. With her class as an audience, Ms. Krauss shared with Mrs. Collins the introduction to a piece she was writing about her son's first word.

Ms. Krauss: I'm stuck. This is something I really want to write about, but now I'm stuck. The introduction is boring. I haven't made Roger's first word sound at all interesting.

Mrs. Collins: Why do you want to tell this story so badly?

Ms. Krauss: Well, Tim [*Ms. Krauss' husband*] missed the first time Roger stood up. And then he missed his first steps. Now he's missed Roger's first word. So I wanted to write something Tim would like to read.

Mrs. Collins: Maybe you could write this as a letter to Tim.

Ms. Krauss: Hmm. That's an idea. I'm going to think about this some more. Thanks for talking to me about this.

Ms. Krauss then summarized the purpose of this minilesson for her students. She said, "Even the best writers sometimes get stuck, but talking to someone else about what they're writing can help. So if you get stuck when you're writing, try talking to someone. It might help you get unstuck."

Several weeks later, Ms. Krauss followed up on this minilesson. She asked her students to share their experiences of talking about their writing with other children and adults. She was pleased when Alex, a student who rarely wrote much, explained how talking to his friend Todd helped him find something to write about.

Other writing strategies we've seen teachers demonstrate through minilessons include different approaches to brainstorm writing topics; writers' notebooks to collect writing ideas; and various strategies to help students revise their writing. For example, Laura Harper (1997) used minilessons to demonstrate to her students a range of revision strategies that specifically responded to the problems she regularly encountered in their writing. She chose strategies that would encourage students to expand "exciting moments" in their stories; to offer more details about characters and settings in their writing; to add information about the "internal landscapes" of characters; and to assess the proportion of text devoted to character development, plot, setting, and so on.

The use of graphic organizers to help students think about how to plan and organize their writing is another strategy teachers can demonstrate through minilessons to support struggling writers (Graham, Harris, and MacArthur 1993). For instance, Lisa Fink (n.d.) authored a series of lessons using story maps to help students identify common elements of fairy tales (see Figure 3.2), a strategy that students could use to organize the writing of their own fairy tales. These lessons include links to interactive story maps for characters, setting, conflict, and resolution that can be filled in online or printed and copied for student use. The character story map, for example, asks students to indicate what each character looks like; how characters act; and how other characters react to each character. The story map for conflict asks students to describe the setting and where and when the story took place.

We've also seen teachers use minilessons to show students how to use semantic maps to make associations between concepts and words they may explore in their writing. This is a useful strategy for many struggling writers, who often benefit from structures that help organize their writing (Graham, Harris, and Troia 2000). For example,

Figure 3.2 Common Elements of Fairy Tales

- Do NOT need to include fairies.
- Set in the past—usually significantly long ago. May be presented as historical fact from the past.
- Include fantasy, supernatural, or make-believe aspects.
- Typically incorporate clearly defined good characters and evil characters.
- Involve magic elements, which may be magical people, animals, or objects. May be positive or negative.
- May include objects, people, or events in threes.
- Focus the plot on a problem of conflict that needs to be solved.
- Often have happy endings, based on the resolution of the conflict.
- Usually teach a lesson or demonstrate values important to the culture.

Source: readwritethink.org

to prepare to write narrative fiction, students may create a semantic map by responding to the following questions:

- What will the story be about?
- What will happen in the story?
- Who are the characters in the story?
- Where will the story take place?

During a whole-class minilesson, teachers could work with their class to create one large semantic map based on these questions, or they could create separate maps for each question.

The potential of semantic mapping is not limited to fairy tales or narrative fiction. Mr. Gorka, a second-grade teacher, created a mini-lesson to demonstrate the use of semantic mapping to plan a piece he wanted to write for his class to recount his experiences during a trip he and his wife had taken to New Mexico the previous summer. Over the course of a couple of minilessons, he created the semantic map shown in Figure 3.3 to plan and organize the story of his trip to New Mexico.

This is a good place to make an important point: *effective writing teachers teach writing, not strategies.* It seems to us that sometimes prewriting strategies such as graphic organizers are taught as though this exercise was the point of learning to write—that mastery of these strategies indicated evidence of writing skill. However, when teachers demonstrate the use of graphic organizers during a minilesson, they are actually illustrating a strategy that *some* writers use *some* of the time to plan and organize their writing. No writers use graphic organizers all of the time, and many writers, such as Curt Dudley-Marling, never use them at all. Nor does teaching the use of graphic organizers ensure that students will actually use them in the context of their own writing (Graham, Harris, and MacArthur 1993). Rather, the point of demonstrating the use of graphic organizers or other organizational strategies is to show students that effective writers make plans and organize their work in some way. Effective writers may not all use graphic organizers, but they generally give some thought in advance to what they're going to write, how they're going to organize their writing, and so on. Plans may change but they usually exist, and the effectiveness of different planning strategies for different writers usually depends on their purposes for writing, their anticipated audiences, and their personal preferences.

A Classroom Teacher's Guide to Struggling Writers

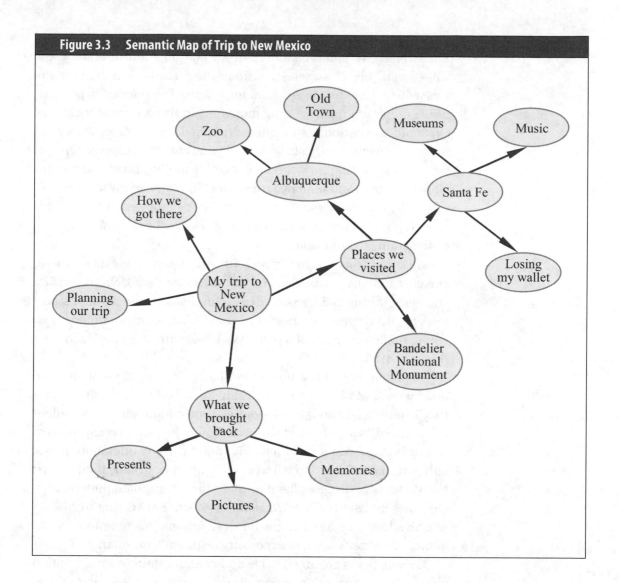

Figure 3.3   Semantic Map of Trip to New Mexico

Discussions/Peer Lessons

Writing expertise does not just reside in the heads of teachers; it is distributed throughout the classroom. In classrooms as early as first grade, we've seen teachers ask students to lead brief minilessons on punctuation they have recently mastered, spelling patterns they have discovered, or other breakthroughs they have made in their writing. For instance, Jennifer, a student in Mr. Seeger's fourth-grade class, shared with her classmates revisions she'd made to a memoir she was writing. Jennifer talked about how she had responded to peer critiques of her writing by adding more details about various incidents. On another occasion, a struggling writer in the same class shared the process he went through to write a Big Book for the kindergarten students, emphasizing how the audience for the Big Book affected his choice of words and sentence structures. Similarly, many teachers occasionally use minilessons to have students share writing topics; this models possible ideas for students who are having difficulty thinking of something to write about.

We know other teachers who routinely engage students in whole-class discussions of samples of student writing to talk about revision strategies during minilessons. For example, with the student's permission, third-grade teacher Stephanie Collins shared with her class copies of the first page of a piece Mark had written about Halloween (Figure 3.4).

Stephanie began the minilesson by asking her students to read quietly what Mark had written. Then she asked them to share what they had noticed about Mark's piece. Almost immediately, a student commented, "He didn't use any periods. Readers aren't going to know where to stop." Another added, "He didn't use any quotation marks, either. It makes it hard to tell who's talking." Ms. Collins then invited her students to discuss where to place the appropriate punctuation. On other occasions she used samples of student writing to discuss effective leads, detailed character descriptions, paragraphing, word choice, the organization of expository texts, and grammar.

Overall, peers are an effective and credible source of information about the craft of writing, especially for struggling writers whose relationships with teachers have often been strained by the stress of academic failure.

Shared and Interactive Writing

Many teachers use minilessons as opportunities to engage students in collaborative writing. Shared writing, in which students dictate texts and teachers function as scribes, for example, develops confidence and motivation for struggling writers. It also models the writing

A Classroom Teacher's Guide to Struggling Writers

Figure 3.4 Mark's Story About Halloween

(1) MARK aND CORWININ IN THe
HanTeD HoUSe
ONeDay CORWin aND MaRK weRe
HoMe PLaYinG SUPeR NinTenDO anD
THe GaMe WaS CoLLeD SuPeR MaRIO
WORLD aND THen aRe PaReNTS
CaMe in aND SaID To Go UP STaRS
aND DoaRe CHcRS So THen We
WeNT UP STaRS So THen MaRK SaID
WHaT DO YOU THink aBOUT THUT
HoUSe a CRcSS THe STReeT
WHaT DO YOU MeaN SaID CORWin
WeLL JUST LOOK aT iT SaiD MaRK
I THink THaT HoUSe iS HaUNTeNN
WHY SaiD CORWin WeLL EVRY
NiGHT IV BeeN LOOKinG OUT THO
WinDOW aND THe LIGHTS WeRe TURNinG
On aND OFF aND I aLSO SaW SHaDOWS
in THe HoUSe SaiD MaRK aND aFOPeL
OF NiGHTS a Go I WoKe aT MICNiGHT
aND I HeRD SCReeMS SaID MaRK
aRe YoU SuRe CORWin SaID OF CoReS
Im SuRe MaRK SaiD BU+ WHY aRe
YoU TeLLiNG Me THiS CORWin SaiD
BeCaUSe SaiD MaRK I THink We SHOLD
Go OVeR TO MOROW DO YoU ReLLeY
MeaN iT CORWin SaiD WHaT
DO YOU THink MaRkSaID WOULD
YOU LiKe To CoMe WiTH Me CORWin
MaRkSaiD WeLL I GUSS SO CORWin
SaID BUT WHaT TiMe CORWin SaiD
LeTS LeVe TO MORROWinafTeR NooN
SCOOL BUT WHY aRe We GOinG
aFTeR SCOOL CORWin SaiD BeCaUSe
We HaVe SCOOL TO MORRCW
DUMMY,

process in action. Typically, teachers invite students to suggest text on particular topics—such as a recount of a field trip, a thank-you note, directions to make something, or a short piece of fiction—and the teacher records their contributions on an overhead transparency or chart paper. Mrs. Ebberhard, a second-grade teacher, invited her students to dictate directions for making a peanut butter and jelly sandwich. When they were done, she tried to make the sandwich by following their directions. As confusion arose, the students realized they needed to refine their writing. This process forced students to consider the reader's need for sufficiently explicit instructions.

Interactive writing—sometimes referred to as "sharing the pen"—is a type of shared writing that provides students with an authentic means for instruction in phonics and other linguistic patterns within the context of real, meaningful texts (Button, Johnson, and Furgerson 1996). As they do for shared writing, teachers invite students to contribute to a collaborative text, which teachers transcribe on chart paper or an overhead transparency. However, for interactive writing, teachers explicitly model rules for conventional spelling, punctuation, and grammar—all important issues for students who struggle with their writing—in meaningful contexts. Button, Johnson, and Furgerson (1996) suggest a variety of questions teachers might pose as students suggest sentences for the teacher to transcribe:

- How many words are there in our sentence?
- Where (on the page) do we begin writing?
- Say the word slowly. What sounds do you hear?
- What letter of the alphabet stands for that sound?
- What comes at the end of our sentence?
- Could someone point to and read what we've written so far? (449)

Of course, the kinds of questions teachers ask or what skills they choose to model will be a function of children's general developmental level. Again, teachers should make every effort to avoid teaching skills students have already mastered.

Explicit Teaching

We've emphasized that all writers, particularly struggling writers, benefit from explicit instruction. Modeling, demonstrations, and discussions are all important, but often it is necessary for teachers to augment these instructional strategies with more explicit teaching. For instance, following a whole-class discussion of punctuation and spelling, teachers may need to conduct brief minilessons in which they explicitly teach rules for conventional spelling or punctuation.

A Classroom Teacher's Guide to Struggling Writers

After a whole-class discussion on the use of quotation marks to represent dialogue, Tammy Carter, a third-grade teacher, did a brief minilesson to show students where periods typically go when they use direct quotes in their writing. To begin, she used a phrase from an actual piece of student writing, which she wrote on chart paper:

Mike said "Look out below".

She commented, "The writer did a good job here taking the words Mike said and putting quotation marks on either side of them. She also put a period at the end of the sentence, which is also good. But there is a rule about this that you ought to know: If quotations come at the end of the sentence, the period goes inside of the quotation marks." She used an arrow to indicate moving the period from outside to inside the quotation marks. She continued, "Here's the rule: When a quote comes at the end of a sentence, the period goes inside the quotation marks." She wrote the rule on the chart paper, which she later posted on a wall in the back of the classroom.

Over the course of the school year, Tammy conducted explicit minilessons on several types of punctuation, unusual spelling patterns, paragraphing, forms of address in letters and emails, sentence combination, pronoun use, and so on. Importantly, these minilessons always supplemented other lessons that focused on modeling, demonstrations, and discussions, and Tammy often followed up with individual writing conferences and small-group lessons.

Explicit instruction is useful for teaching writing skills and strategies to struggling writers, including students who are learning English as an additional language and do not bring an intrinsic acquired knowledge of the language structures to their literacy learning. It is worth mentioning, however, that explicit instruction should not be used to teach prescriptive writing processes. In other words, it is harmful to teach a writing process—for instance, brainstorm, prewrite, write, revise, publish—as though *all writers* utilize the *same process* for *all kinds of writing*. Teaching writing as prescriptions will only make learning to write more difficult (Labbo, Hoffman, and Roser 1995). In general, teachers must focus on helping writers learn strategies and processes they find useful in fulfilling *their* intentions with projected audiences. Not all writers find the same strategies and processes useful.

Minilessons that Address the Qualities of Good Writing

In Chapter 1, we stressed that published authors are among our best teachers of writing. This is why many teachers rely on children's literature to illustrate various literary elements, such as theme, characterization, figurative language, imagery, tone, and perspective, or particular language features students might use in their writing. Mr. Wheeler, for example, used *The Name Jar* (Choi 2001) during a minilesson to illustrate how character development contributes to shaping the plot. After previewing the book by looking at and discussing the illustrations to gain a general understanding of the story and then reading it aloud, he invited his students to create a list of the characters and brainstorm their qualities. As students shared, Mr. Wheeler used a chart to map the characters and their attributes. The students then looked for language the author employed to communicate those attributes, which Mr. Wheeler entered in the chart (see Figure 3.5). At the conclusion of the minilesson, Mr. Wheeler encouraged students to think about how they might use language to communicate attributes in their own writing.

Special education teacher Dorothy Gilday created a minilesson using *Click, Clack, Moo* (Cronin and Lewin 2000) to illustrate how authors use "connector words" to create a coherent text. She first read—and then reread—*Click, Clack, Moo,* asking her students to notice words that the author used to help readers track the sequence of events. Ms. Gilday and her students then created the following list of words and phrases that indicated the sequence of action in *Click, Clack, Moo*:

- All day long . . .
- At first . . .
- Then . . .
- The next day . . .
- All night long . . .
- Early next morning . . .
- The next morning . . .

Ms. Gilday concluded the minilesson by asking students to explore using connector words during writing workshop. She also followed up on this minilesson with individual writing conferences and small-

Figure 3.5 Character Attribute Chart	
Characters	**Qualities and Text Examples**
Unhei (main character)	Scared and nervous in new situation, thoughtful, questioning, friendly, reflective
	Text example showing Unhei as thoughtful and reflective: Unhei looked out the window and saw it was sprinkling. *It's the same rain*, she thought, *but in a different place.*
Unhei's grandmother	Advocate, loving, concerned, anticipates what will happen in new country
	Text example: As she ran her fingers along the grooves and ridges of the Korean characters, she pictured her grandmother's smile.
Kids on the bus	Teasing, mean to new kid, mean because they didn't understand
	Text example: "Oh, it's Yoo-hey," the boy said. "Like 'You hey!' What about 'Hey, you!' "
Unhei's mother	Strong supporter of Unhei to be a good student, affirming of Korean heritage, good listener
	Text example: "You *are* different, Unhei," her mother said. "That's a good thing!"
Mr. Kim (store clerk)	Kind, helpful, gentle, affirming of Korean heritage
	Text example: "Ahh, what a beautiful name," he said. "Doesn't it mean *grace*?" "A graceful name for a graceful girl," Mr. Kim said.

group lessons to ensure that students understood how to use connector words and when they can be useful.

Summary

As we noted in Chapter 1, writing workshops have been criticized for not teaching the skills of writing of writing. However, teaching struggling students to write must include explicit attention to the skills and strategies used by effective writers. As we also noted in Chapter 1, laissez faire teaching is always bad teaching. In the context of a writing workshop, five- to ten-minute minilessons provide opportunities for teachers to teach the routines of the writing workshop, the skills and strategies used by effective writers, and to illustrate the qualities of good writing. Independent writing time, the topic of the following chapter, provides extended periods of time for students to practice the skills of writing they learned during workshop minilessons and for teachers to provide additional skill instruction in the context of individual and small-group writing conferences.

Independent Writing and Whole-Class Sharing

What Students and Teachers Do

Independent writing time provides opportunities for teachers to provide struggling writers with the *frequent, intensive, explicit,* and *individualized support and direction* they need through the use of individual writing conferences and small-group work. As well, the independent writing period provides struggling writers with significant blocks of time to practice the craft of writing, putting to use what they've learned in whole-class minilessons, small-group lessons, and individual writing conferences. During the independent writing period, students can also share their writing with their peers in order to get authentic responses to their work. This action helps students determine if their writing is effective—that is, how well it fulfills their intentions with this particular audience. Furthermore, struggling writers can also use independent writing time to engage in other writing-related activities that respond to their particular needs.

The independent writing period is also a time when teachers collect the careful, ongoing assessment data that is crucial to ensuring that their instruction responds to the individual needs of struggling writers. Because this is such an essential step for the effective teaching of writing, we discuss assessment as a separate issue in Chapter 7.

Although what teachers do cannot be separated from what students do, as a matter of convenience we have organized this section in terms of *what students do* and *what teachers do* during independent writing time.

What Students Do

Providing students with significant blocks of time for independent writing is crucial to the writing development of all students, particularly struggling writers, who often spend less time writing than their peers and more time practicing decontextualized skills such as spelling and grammar.

Personal Investment in Writing

Donald Graves (1983) has made the case that students are far more likely to work with a piece of writing if they have some personal investment in the topics of their writing. Dudley-Marling and Oppenheimer (1995) found that seventh- and eighth-grade students who had little control over the form and content of their writing rarely did any sort of revision beyond making surface-level changes recommended by their teachers. In general, students who write for purposes and audiences of interest to them are more likely to engage in writing in the first place, and they are more willing to edit and revise their writing to make it more effective. Allowing students to link writing to their experiences and interests will help struggling writers "see themselves officially as writers and . . . [allows] teachers more footholds from which to build—more ways of engaging children in classroom literacy events" (Dyson and Freedman 2003, 970).

We've been clear about our belief that struggling writers need to write for a range of purposes and audiences and to exercise some control over the form and content of their writing. But how much control should students have? There are a variety of principled approaches to organizing independent writing that honor student ownership and recognize the need for pushing students to write widely. For instance, many teachers organize their writing instruction around genre studies. First-grade teacher Gary McPhail (2008), for example, focused on three writing genres over the course of the academic year: narrative fiction, comic books, and poetry. During each unit of study, students worked exclusively within that genre, but still exercised some control over the content of their writing. Of course, it was expected that teachers in subsequent grades would emphasis other genres.

We know other teachers who offer students considerable latitude over both the form and content of their writing. These teachers rely on minilessons and writing conferences to encourage students to explore different writing genres. But sometimes teachers insist that students try a different genre or topic. When he taught third grade, Curt Dudley-Marling told several of his struggling writers to move beyond collaborative "buddy" stories and try something else. He then helped them brainstorm other possible topics. On a related issue, teachers may sometimes need to prohibit writing topics that are offensive or hurtful. Still, teachers need to be exceedingly cautious about banning writing topics merely because they make them uncomfortable. Newkirk (2002) has documented how restrictions on writing topics, such as bans on even mild forms of violence, can discourage some students from writing at all.

Other teachers combine genre study and open-format approaches to independent writing. For example, one fourth-grade teacher does three six-week genre studies (Big Books, memoir, and poetry) over the course of the year. The rest of the year, students can write in any genre they wish.

Finally, there is one reality that will always limit students' ownership of their writing: on-demand, high-stakes writing assessments. High-stakes testing demands that teachers give students some practice writing in genres—and on topics—that will prepare them to succeed on the test. Some portion of writing time over the course of the school year will almost certainly be devoted to writing to prompts as the tests approach. This isn't a problem as long as preparing for the tests doesn't limit students' opportunities to write for other purposes and audiences. Students who have a strong sense of how to vary the form and content of their writing according to their purposes and audiences will have relatively little difficulty learning the genre of high-stakes writing tests.

Collaborative Writing

The writing process is usually portrayed as a solitary activity. However, in many writing workshops, students sometimes create texts collaboratively. Allowing for the possibility of collaborative writing acknowledges that writing is an inherently social process that "entails learning to differentiate and manipulate the elements of the written system (e.g., letters and words) in order to engage with, and manipulate, the social world" (Dyson 2001, 126). Many struggling writers are more motivated to write when they are able to use writing to build and maintain social relationships (Dudley-Marling 1997; Dyson 1993). For example, in Mrs. Mitchell's writing workshop (discussed in Chapter 2), boys often worked together in groups of up to four students to write adventure stories that included themselves as characters. Some of the girls also produced collaborative texts, usually retrospective accounts that celebrated their friendships.

We've seen students work together during independent writing time to write chants, poems for two voices, songs, plays, and class newspapers. Drama and writing in role (e.g., an eight-year-old girl writing from the perspective of an adolescent boy), in particular, "have tremendous possibilities for both tapping students' imaginations and helping them resituate themselves" (Chapman 1999, 480). By writing in role, "students put themselves into different situations, see things from different perspectives, and situate themselves differently in relation to other times, places, and people" (Chapman 1999, 480). Writing in role may be especially powerful for struggling writers who have difficulty adjusting the form and content of their writing according to the needs of their audiences.

Collaborative writing allows struggling writers to benefit from models provided by more capable writers, but such collaborations are not to the detriment of the more capable writers. In our experience, accomplished writers, because they have to make explicit their own decision-making processes, also benefit from collaborations with struggling writers. Therefore, we recommend that teachers give all students the opportunity to write collaboratively during independent writing time. (See Cohen 1994 for strategies to ensure that all students benefit from small-group work, regardless of their ability levels.)

A Classroom Teacher's Guide to Struggling Writers

Peer Conferences

Talk is a critical component of the writing process, even for the most skilled writers. Therefore, effective writing teachers build into independent writing time opportunities for students to talk about their writing with their peers. Peer conferences give struggling writers a chance to solicit peer assistance when they're stuck or to get feedback on a piece of writing in progress. Alternately, they might ask a classmate for help with a particular writing convention or to find "just the right word." Peers can also function as editors to help their classmates get a piece of writing ready to share with wider audiences. However, students need to be taught how to respond to each other's writing. In our experience, peer conferences frequently fail to respond to writers' needs. Too often, requests for feedback on writing in progress merely elicit feedback on writing conventions and other surface-level features, ignoring the fundamental question: Is the writing likely to fulfill the writer's intention (to persuade, for example) with the intended audience?

If teachers want their students to participate in peer conferences, we recommend that they explicitly teach students how to respond to someone else's writing, a process that focuses specifically on what the writer is trying to do and with whom. This is particularly important for struggling writers, who may be reluctant to write for fear of harsh feedback. Response should also consider the kind of feedback the writer would like at particular stages of the writing process. Sometimes writers just want someone to *hear* their writing, with little response beyond "I like it" or "that makes sense." Therefore, teachers should teach student writers how to indicate the kind of response they'd like, and remind peers that they should provide only the kind of feedback that's desired (or needed).

In general, teachers provide powerful models of the kind of responses their students will give to each other's writing. If a teacher's feedback on students' writing focuses mainly on issues of correctness, or if the teacher often attempts to control of students' writing (through responses such as "this is the what I'd write" or "this is the way I'd say it"), then students will usually do the same. Alternatively, if teachers respond to what young writers are trying to do and provide the kind of feedback they would like at particular stages of the writing process, then students will likely follow suit.

Other Writing Activities

The aim of independent writing time is to provide students with extended periods of time to write texts, to engage in the processes of effective writing, and to practice skills and strategies learned in mini-lessons and writing conferences. There may, however, be occasions when struggling writers can profitably engage in writing-related activities targeted to helping students attend to specific writing skills or strategies. For example, particular students may benefit from word sorts that encourage them to focus on specific spelling patterns; others may benefit from sentence-combining exercises to prompt them to write more complex sentences. Creating a semantic map of word derivations, such as *graph, photograph, photography, photographer,* and so forth, is another example of a potentially useful activity.

At the same time, it's important to note that we believe such activities should be used judiciously. Struggling writers need more time—not less—to write than many of their peers and, to the degree that writing-related activities deprive struggling writers of writing time, these activities can be detrimental to their development as writers.

Writing-related activities also include all the things writers do to prepare to write: conducting research, taking notes, brainstorming topics, and so forth. During independent writing time, a student who plans to describe the process of making ice cream will have to spend some time searching for information by consulting various print and Web-based resources. Another student may spend his time jotting down notes to help him think about what he's going to write. A student editing her work may consult a dictionary to check on spellings, or she may search for a book that contains examples of punctuation use she finds confusing. And, of course, students will spend some of their time talking to classmates and teachers about their writing.

What Teachers Do

While students are working independently, teachers have the time they need to work with struggling writers individually and in small groups to teach the skills, strategies, and processes of effective writing.

A Classroom Teacher's Guide to Struggling Writers

Writing Conferences

During writing conferences, teachers are able to address the specific needs of struggling writers. Sometimes teachers conduct brief conferences to check in with students to see how they're doing and if there are any problems. Perhaps a student is stuck and requires guidance to keep writing. A brief conference may be sufficient to push the student to move on to a different topic or to try out a new genre. Or the teacher may just want to meet briefly with students to keep track of what they are writing. Another student may request a quick writing conference because she is struggling to find an engaging topic. These sorts of mini-conferences may take only a minute or two.

More often, teachers use writing conferences to teach the skills of effective writing by working with students to help them shape a particular piece of writing. These conferences may last as long as ten minutes, but teachers should be careful not to allow these conferences to go too long since all students require some measure of individual support and direction. Struggling writers will require more individualized support, but teachers cannot afford to ignore the needs of other students. As well, overly long conferences can create discipline problems. For struggling students who need additional attention, it's better to conduct a series of conferences over the course of the week. If a teacher holds a conference with a struggling writer for five to six minutes a day, for example, over the course of a week, this student will have had up to thirty minutes of individual support and direction.

To select a focus for the conference, a teacher must begin with the fundamental assessment question: Does the student's writing work to fulfill her intention(s) with her imagined audiences in specific social contexts? Next, the teacher must ask: What does this student need to learn to make the writing more effective? Doe the writer need to pay more attention to the needs of the audience? To include more details? Perhaps the issue is punctuation and grammar.

More than likely, each piece of writing will include multiple issues, and the teacher will need to prioritize the skills and strategies to address during the conference. Teaching too many skills or strategies at once risks paralyzing students, especially struggling writers, so setting priorities is important. At the same time, teachers must avoid the trap of focusing on lower-level skills with struggling readers (Glasswell,

Parr, and McNaughton 2003). For all writers, the priority should be on the skills and strategies that will have the most impact on the piece of writing the student is currently working on. Focusing on spelling and punctuation, for example, may have less impact on the efficacy of a student's writing than helping that writer think more about the needs of the audience. At other times, mechanics may indeed be the most productive focus.

Whatever the conference's focus, teachers must respond to what students are trying to do, not what they're trying to teach (Labbo, Hoffman, and Roser 1995). In other words, the emphasis must be on the student's intention(s) and intended audience. The following example shows a conference between a third-grade teacher, Mary Moran, and Edgar, a struggling writer who was working on a book "for next year's third graders" about the class garden. She began by asking him to read his piece to her. Here's what Edgar had written so far:

> On this chapter I'm going to show my experiences it is about gardening. I never gardened before. When we go outside to make observation my illustratashens are good if you want to see the pictures Mrs. Moran will have my book.
> Some jobs were hard. Some things were exciting. Something surprised me the first radish came out and the lettuce is bigger.

Based on her ongoing assessment of Edgar's writing, Ms. Moran had already determined that Edgar needed to learn to include additional details to make his writing more effective. Edgar routinely provided this kind of detail in his drawings and in conversations with classmates about the class garden, so here she decided to push Edgar to elaborate on what he meant by the words *surprised* and *hard*. She started the discussion by asking him a few questions:

Ms. Moran: Remember when we organized our experiences on the chart? When you are describing, there are words that help your description come alive. So, can you think of a way to describe why you were surprised by the radish?

Edgar: Well, it just popped out overnight, right under the soil.

Ms. Moran: What did it look like?

Edgar: It looked like a little red marble.

Ms. Moran: Let's see, can we write this down?

With her help, Edgar wrote, "The first radish popped out and it looked like a little red marble." To prompt Edgar to elaborate on his own, she asked him to explain further.

Ms. Moran: So you say here that *some jobs were hard.* What was hard?

Edgar: It was hard because we had to carry compost.

Ms. Moran: You have a lot of information here. Maybe you can split it up.

She wrote a sentence starter on the next page of Edgar's notebook: *The hard part was carrying the compost because . . .*

Ms. Moran: If you are going to say *surprising* or *hard*, please explain these words further.

Back at his desk, Edgar revised his draft a bit more. When the class lined up for computer period, he wanted to keep going. Before Edgar left the classroom, he eagerly read his revision to Ms. Moran:

> We planted lettuce first and the radishes are growing more then [sic] the lettuce. The first radish just popped out and it looked like a little red marble. Some jobs were hard. The hard part was carrying the compost because it was heavy and hard to carry the compost when we carry it to the trees because it was so hot. The exciting part was watering the plants because when it was hot some water wets you.

Over the next several days, Edgar continued to work on his revision, sharing with Ms. Moran and getting additional feedback from his classmates. When he was satisfied that it was ready, he "published" his work by adding the final edited copy of his chapter to his garden book.

In the conference shown here, Mrs. Moran responded to her assessment of Edgar's writing by helping him add details to make his writing more effective and engaging for his intended audience: next year's third graders. In other writing conferences, she worked with students on word choice, effective leads and conclusions, character development, audience, word choice, transitions, organization, paragraphing, punctuation, revision, syntax, spelling, and so on. If it was appropriate to the student at the time, she sometimes used her writing conferences to follow up on issues she had raised in minilessons. She always tried to respond to what students were trying to do with their writing without engaging in negative evaluation or excessive correction. She knew that although she would have to give each of her students a grade for language arts, negative evaluation frustrates struggling writers (Farnan and Dahl 2003).

Overall, Mrs. Moran's goal for writing conferences was to engage her students in "interactively guided composing, in which ideas are exchanged, elaborated, and integrated" (Dyson and Freedman 2003, 971). In this way, she was able to teach them the skills, strategies, and processes of effective writing.

Finally, Mrs. Moran recognized that research indicates that teachers are, on average, more likely to tolerate interruptions when they are working with struggling writers (Glasswell, Parr, and McNaughton 2003). Therefore, she made sure that her students did not interrupt her conferences. For students who felt they needed immediate help, she posted a sign up sheet with the heading, "I'd like a conference today." She let the class know that when she was available, she would make those conferences a priority.

Teachers like Mrs. Moran recognize that conferencing is an art. There are no formulas for effective conferences. Everyone talks about the use of writing conferences to scaffold struggling writers. People also assume that struggling writers need "sturdier scaffolding" (Glasswell, Parr, and McNaughton 2003). But precisely what this looks like isn't always so clear. Certainly there isn't a prescription for effective writing conferences; indeed, a scripted format could never respond to the individual needs of struggling writers. What's needed is an "inquiry stance" toward writing conferences (Cochran-Smith and Lytle 1999) in which teachers ask, "What is the effect of my writing conferences?" How, for instance, do students respond to writing conferences? Do they make substantive revisions that make their writing more effective, or do they merely make superficial changes to please their teachers? If conferences aren't making a difference in the quality of student writing, what's the problem?

It takes time to learn to conduct effective writing conferences. But the mere passage of time will not make teachers good at conferencing. Teachers need to carefully examine the quality of their interactions with students during writing conferences and the effect of these conferences on students' writing. We recommend that teachers routinely audiotape their writing conferences and then listen to at least some of the recordings. We know some teachers who play back their writing conferences on the way home in their cars. Ideally, teachers may choose to work together to study and improve their conferencing and writing program in general. In any case, the ability to reflect on their practice may be the most important trait of effective teachers of writing.

Additional Writing Activities

Teachers can also work with students individually and in small groups to teach the craft of writing by engaging students in other sorts of writing activities. Some struggling writers are reluctant to do much writing at all, so teachers might use individual lessons to engage them in writing activities designed to "prime the pump." Teachers could, for example, ask a student to do a *free write*, in which the student writes nonstop for ten minutes without worrying about punctuation, spelling, or even meaning. If a student can't think of anything to write during the free write, teachers can suggest writing whatever comes to mind, even if it's the phrase "I don't know what to write." The goal of free writing is simply to get students more comfortable with the act of writing without additional concerns about the audience or final grade.

Teachers can also ask reluctant writers to do a *quick write*: to write for one or two minutes about their response to an activity or event. They could even ask students to write about how they feel about being asked to do a quick write.

A *written conversation* is a particularly inviting way to engage reluctant writers in writing. A written conversation is literally a conversation carried on by two or more people in writing, but, unlike Instant Messaging, the participants are usually sitting next to each other. The following example is excerpted from a written conversation that took place between Mike, a reluctant writer, and Ms. Maines, his teacher.

Ms. Maines: Mike, I heard you went to Revere Beach on Sunday.

Mike: I went with my mom and dad and my little sister.

Ms. Maines: What did you do at the beach?

Mike: Swim and stuff.

Ms. Maines: How was the water?

Mike: Cold. But it was realy hot. My sister woldnt go in.

Ms. Maines: She wouldn't go in? Was it too cold for her?

Mike: Yes.

Ms. Maines: Anything else you can tell me about your day at the beach?

Mike: We ate rost beef sandwichs from Kellys.

Ms. Maines: I love Kelly's roast beef sandwiches.

Written conversations encourage writing and also give teachers the opportunity to model conventional spelling and punctuation. In the final turn between Ms. Maines and Mike, Ms. Maines was able to model conventional spelling for *roast* and *sandwiches* and the possessive form for *Kelly's.*

Teachers can also use shared and interactive writing to encourage reluctant writers. In some cases, teachers may invite individual students to dictate language experience stories or other texts to get students started.

Opportunities for Students to Share Writing

We've stressed that writers always begin with a purpose and an intended audience. We have also argued that the effectiveness of any piece of writing can only be determined by gauging audience response. The *proof of the pudding* is in the writer's effect on readers. For this reason, most teachers provide some space within the structure of writing workshop for students to share their writing with classmates or wider audiences. Sharing their writing gives young writers opportunities to see if their writing *works.*

Author's Chair

One way to invite students to share their writing is the Author's Chair (Graves 1983, 1994). Typically, teachers ask, "Who would like to share their writing today?" and invite one or two children to share a finished piece of writing or a piece of writing in progress with the whole class. The Author's Chair responds to young authors' need for attentive listeners. Therefore, the emphasis must be on an authentic response that attends to the writers' need to find out what their classmates understand or do not understand in their texts (Graves 1994).

A Classroom Teacher's Guide to Struggling Writers

Graves is critical, however, of *pro forma* responses to students in the Author's Chair, including audience statements such as "I like . . ."; questions from the author such as, "What's your favorite part?"; and questions to the author such as "What will you write next?" He also discourages routine clapping after each piece is read.

For children to provide a supportive response to their classmate's writing, Graves argues that they must first take the time to think about what they've heard. He suggests that students can initially respond to their classmate's writing by offering "remembers," which connect the writer's experience with those of the audience (e.g., "that reminds me of the time my dog got lost"). The teacher can step in to make sure the audience has connected with the author's intentions by asking the writer, "Are there important parts of your story that we missed?" (Graves 1994, 134).

After this reflection and connection, children should focus their feedback on their genuine response to the author's intention. Did it make sense to them? Were they confused? Did they feel there were sufficient details? Did the ordering of ideas make sense to them? Did the piece accomplish what the author hoped for? For example, if the author planned to write a humorous piece, did they find it funny? At this point, students can ask the author questions about passages they didn't understand. Again, teachers must model—and, in some cases, explicitly teach children—how to respond supportively to students in the Author's Chair.

Teachers must also take responsibility for summarizing students' feedback for young authors and translating the responses into useful advice. For example, Zecker, Pappas, and Cohen (1998) quote one teacher's summary of the class' feedback: "These questions . . . make me think, Raúl, that sometimes it is good to give more details. The audience wants more information. Maybe next time you can give more details" (248).

There are no formulas for Author's Chair. Therefore, teachers need to regularly reflect on the efficacy of student response and, if necessary, work with their students to teach them how to provide more effective responses to their classmates' writing.

Not every piece of student writing needs be shared, and not all students will be comfortable sharing with the whole class. No student should be forced to share during Author's Chair (Labbo, Hoffman, and Roser 1995). Teachers can, however, ask students who are reluctant to share in the large group to find one or more students to share their writing with during independent writing time (Graves 1994).

Publishing

In many classrooms, teachers encourage students to "publish" their writing to share with classmates or other students in the school. It's fairly common in elementary classrooms across the country to see children's writing displayed in book form for classmates to read. We've even seen students' work displayed in school libraries where anyone can check it out. The formal sharing of student writing in this way celebrates their accomplishments but also provides an opportunity for young authors to see how readers respond to their work—that is, was it effective? If students wrote a Big Book for young readers, did the readers find the book engaging? If students produced a class newspaper, how did their classmates respond?

Publishing student writing to share with a wider audience raises questions about whether children's writing should be edited before it is published. In general, we think it is desirable for teachers (or classroom volunteers) to edit students' writing before it is disseminated. After all, even commercially produced books—including this book—have the benefit of copyediting. Editing children's work makes it more readable and effective. It also spares children (and perhaps teachers) unnecessary embarrassment. Editors should not, however, make any edits that threaten the writer's intention. For this reason, it may be prudent to give students the right of final approval over editorial changes.

As a matter of principle, teachers should always encourage students to write for real audiences. Children who write in journals benefit from teachers who read and respond to their entries. Children's letters actually ought to be sent and, hopefully, responded to. How-to pieces ought to be tried out. Student-written plays should be performed. Book reports can be sent to students in other classes or schools by email or conventional post. Technologies such as email and Instant Messaging provide opportunities for nearly instantaneous responses to students' writing. In general, writing for real audiences gives young writers a chance to test out whether or not their writing *works.*

Summary

There is an uneven relationship between learning *about* something and learning *how* to do it. Learning about the skills of writing, for example, is poor preparation for learning how to write, a problem that often plagues writing instruction for many struggling writers. A writing workshop offers young writers extended periods of independent writing time to practice the skills, strategies, and processes of effective writing that they learned in minilessons and writing conferences. Moreover, a writing workshop allows students to engage in writing texts in which they have some personal investment with the support and direction of their teachers. A writing workshop also provides students with opportunities to share their writing with authentic audiences, which gives them some indication of the effectiveness of their writing. In the context of a writing workshop, struggling writers have a range of experiences that respond to their individual needs as writers.

5

A Genre Approach to Writing Instruction

Children do not learn to write "once and for all" (Gee 1996). Instead, writers learn to write particular kinds of text, for particular purposes and audiences, in particular (social) situations. Specifically, effective writers learn the vocabulary, sentence structures, organization, style, and conventions (spelling, punctuation) appropriate to particular genres. From this perspective, effective writing is less about mastering "correct" forms than learning to manipulate various (genre) features according to "who wants to write, to or for whom, about what, and why" (Dyson and Freedman 2003, 968). Therefore, students don't learn to *write*; they learn to write particular genres, such as narratives, personal letters, memoirs, expository texts, research reports, and so on. Even then, effective writing isn't simply a matter of slotting forms into appropriate genre models (Chapman 1999). Effective writers don't *master* genre features; they learn to *use* these features flexibly according to their appraisal of their purposes, audiences (including their own relationship to that audience), and the social situations in which they are writing.

Take the example of letter writing. Writers don't write letters by calling forth the genre of letter writing. Particular people (e.g., a young girl, a woman, an old man) in particular roles (e.g., friend, mother, customer) write letters to specific audiences (e.g., best friend, son, customer service representative) for various purposes (e.g., to share personal stories, to communicate bad news, to complain about a product). Who is writing to whom, for what purpose, and under what circumstances affect writers' choices about content, vocabulary, and form—ways of organizing their words and ideas, including spelling, punctuation, and grammar (Chapman 1999). A young girl writing a letter from summer camp to a close friend to share stories and maintain intimacy will make different choices than a teacher writing a letter of inquiry about a job opportunity. What's particularly important here is that neither the young girl nor the teacher set out to write a letter. Instead, they begin with intentions and audiences and then deliberately decide among various modes of expression and associated genres (letters, phone calls, email, text message, and so forth). Ultimately, letter writing isn't a genre form as much as it is a social situation that entails genre features that are different from other social situations—writing a research report, for example—involving audiences and writers with particular intentions.

When we recognize how genres are linked to social situations, we understand why various genre features appropriate to Instant Messaging (unconventional spellings, short responses, limited use of punctuation and capitalization) are unsuitable for school essays (and visa versa). In this example, Instant Messaging and school essays reflect dissimilar social situations involving distinctly different relationships among participants (writers and their audiences) and varying intentions on the part of the writers. This is why claims that sending text and Instant Messages corrupt students' writing miss the point. The mark of skilled writers lies in varying what they say and how they say it—selecting the appropriate genre features—according to the social situation (purpose, audience, social context). Increasingly, choices about "how to say it" include choosing among a wide range of traditional and digital modes of representation. Skilled writers often use features from different genres, creating "hybrid" texts to achieve their purposes.

As Dyson and Freedman (2003) note, construing genres as social situations "characterized by varied components, including setting, participants . . . purposes and goals, message form, content, channel, key or tone, and rules governing the sort of writing . . . that should occur" (969) has important implications for how we teach writing to struggling writers. First, teachers must push struggling writers to attempt a range of genres, recognizing that learning how to write in one genre—narrative fiction, for example—does not automatically transfer to knowledge of how to write in other genres. Further, struggling learners are more likely to learn to use genre features according to the needs of their audiences and their intentions if teachers work to create new situations for using writing—that is, new audiences, purposes, and contexts for writing—rather than teaching new genres as abstract forms (Chapman 1999). This is the problem with the infamous five-paragraph essay, which emphasizes writing form nearly to the exclusion of function. Without an explicit social setting, the audience and purpose of five-paragraph essays are unclear to many students, particularly struggling writers.

Teachers can help struggling students learn to skillfully apply appropriate genre writing across subject areas by providing opportunities for them to write for a broad range of functions. Such teachers provide authentic purposes for academic writing that may include: writing to manage and organize activities, writing descriptions in science observations, using narrative as a tool for extending social studies (biographical accounts), and, generally, being explicit that narrative in language arts is not the only genre worthy of study (Farnan and Dahl 2003).

Also, a genre-focused approach to writing instruction suggests that schools must expand the range of genres taken up with struggling writers in elementary classrooms to reflect the digital literacy practices that are taking on increasing importance outside the classroom and in the workplace. These include searching for information on the Internet and constructing Web pages. At the same time, teachers will find it useful to find a place for nontraditional, out-of-school literacies in the classroom. Instant Messaging, email, and text messaging, for example, can be used to introduce the notion of genre by contrasting features of these popular, out-of-school genres with the features of school-based writing. Drawing on students' out-of-school literacy practices also gives teachers something to build on as they challenge struggling writers to expand the range of purposes and audiences for which they write.

Finally, a genre focus will transform how teachers assess students' writing. Traditionally, students' writing has been evaluated in terms of the presence or absence of particular features—often features associated with specific genres—apart from its rhetorical effect (does it *work*). This approach to writing assessment fails to acknowledge that writing is a social process involving author intentions, audiences, and sociocultural contexts. As a result, it ignores the central question in assessing student writing: *Does the writing work to fulfill the writer's intentions with particular audiences?* If the writing is not effective—that is, it doesn't work—what does the writer need to learn to be more effective? The answer to this latter question is the basis for writing instruction that is targeted to the specific needs of individual students. We'll have a lot more to say about assessment in Chapter 6.

In this chapter we discuss strategies for pushing struggling writers to expand the range of genres within which they write—with a special emphasis on writing academic texts, a particular problem for most struggling learners.

Expanding Students' Writing Horizons

Effective writers are able to fulfill a range of communicative intentions with a variety of audiences in various social contexts. In other words, good writers have mastered many genres. But learning to use the forms of one genre, say narrative fiction, is insufficient preparation for writing other genres. To learn to write effective expository texts, for example, students will need frequent opportunities to write—and read—expository texts with support and direction from their teachers. Expanding the range of purposes and audiences for which struggling writers write expands the chances for them to succeed at some form of writing. For example, most students prefer particular writing genres, and many students find that they don't like some genres at all. Tom Newkirk (2002) reports that many boys (and some girls) prefer writing action stories and expository texts, but they do not like writing about personal feelings. Similarly, some students love to write poetry, but others do not. So we might reasonably expect children to be more effective writing in some genres than others.

First-grade teacher Gary McPhail (2008) worried that the emphasis on narrative fiction in his classroom failed to engage many of his students, particularly the struggling writers in his class, who were mostly males. So Gary expanded his writing program to include two additional genre studies: poetry and comic books. Based on an extended classroom inquiry, he discovered that many of his students who struggled with writing narrative fiction did well writing comic books. Other students did well writing poetry. Some of the students whom Gary considered his best writers, based on their writing of narrative fiction, did not do nearly so well writing comic books or poetry. He concluded that in future years he'll offer his students the opportunity to write for an even wider range of genres so all can have a chance to succeed.

Children's literature is an especially powerful way to invite all students to try out new genres. Several years ago, Curt Dudley-Marling spent some time in a first-grade classroom. Over a period of several days—and with the help of the teacher—he shared poems from Paul Fleischman's wonderful collection, *Joyful Noise: Poems for Two Voices* (2004). After a few days, he asked one of the students to rehearse one of the poems with him so they could read it to the class. The day after their reading, two student volunteers rehearsed and read another one of the poems for two voices. Finally, he invited students to work in pairs to write their own poems for two voices. An example is reproduced in Figure 5.1.

Teachers who read books such as *Sugaring Time* by Kathryn Lasky (1983), which describes the process of making maple syrup from tapping to processing, inspire children to write their own expository texts. Similarly, reading alternative folktales like Robert Munsch's *Paperbag Princess* (1986) or Jon Scieszka and Lane Smith's *The True Story of the Three Little Pigs* (1996) invites students to write their own "fractured fairy tales." In general, deliberately reading a wide range of genres to students encourages them to broaden the purposes and audiences for their writing, and it provides data for children about how different genres work.

Teachers who expand the range of genres for which struggling writers write respond to a problem that plagues writing instruction in many elementary classrooms. In too many classrooms, particularly those in low-performing schools, teachers are required to focus writing instruction on preparing students for the high-stakes writing test. In these classrooms, writing instruction is often limited to writing to prompts, usually focusing on the five-paragraph essay form. We do not object to offering students the chance to practice before a test. However, students who have learned to write for a range of

A Classroom Teacher's Guide to Struggling Writers

Figure 5.1   Poem for Two Voices

THE TOOTLER MAAM
by Mr. Dudley-Marling and Andrea

(First voice)   (Second voice)

The Tootler Maam

                                   The Tootler Maam

She toots in every town

                                   She goes to every town

In the country side

                                   In the country side

She walks like a pig

                                   And she talks like a dog

Listen to her walk, clump, clump

                                   Listen to her talk, ruff, ruff

And this is how we end our poem   And this is how we end our poem

purposes and audiences are already well prepared to treat a high-stake writing assessment as just another genre with a particular purpose and audience. Based on her own research, Julie Wollman-Bonilla (2004) concluded that "teachers needn't teach *to* the test in a narrow, evaluation-focused manner; rather they can develop tools that move students *toward* test-readiness while keeping writing process principles in focus" (510). Not only are students who are prepared to write a range of genres likely to perform better on high-stakes writing tests but, more important, they also will be able to harness the power of writing beyond the classroom.

Writing Academic Texts

Many young writers struggle to learn how to vary what they say and how they say it according to their purposes and the needs of their intended audiences. Learning the more formal "academic" language genres associated with schooling is particularly difficult for struggling writers, especially students whose first language isn't English or who speak nonstandard English dialects. Effective writing instruction for these students begins when teachers value the rich linguistic resources children bring with them to school and then explicitly draw on students' existing language resources to help them learn the academic language valued in school. Teachers who do not value students' "ways with words" will find it difficult to persuade students to value the linguistic ways valued in school.

In this section we present extended lessons that provide students with explicit support and direction for learning the features of academic writing. These lessons can easily fit within the structure of a writing workshop, either as extended, whole-class minilessons or as small-group lessons during independent writing time.

Analyzing Texts

In the following examples, teachers help students figure out how written language functions in particular social contexts. Specifically, they explore these questions:

- How does the author develop "ideas" in the text?
- How does the author use language to encourage specific relationships between text and readers?
- What are the structural features that create a coherent, whole text?

These questions help young authors makes choices at the word, clause, and whole-text levels to achieve particular effects in particular social contexts. Too often genres are taught as templates (e.g., starting with graphic organizers for writing the five-paragraph essay) or grammar is taught without context. In either scenario, students gain little understanding of how various linguistic features are used to achieve particular meanings and effects in specific contexts such as school

A Classroom Teacher's Guide to Struggling Writers

(Schleppegrell and Go 2007). In the examples we share here, teachers offer students insights into the linguistic choices made by effective writers and how students can manipulate language to achieve their own communicative goals.

In these examples, teachers focus on science concepts by using "mentor" or "touchstone" texts (Youngs and Barone 2007) to teach students how authors develop concepts by choosing the language features that best meet their intentions. The structure and content of mentor texts illustrate how authors shape texts for specific purposes and contexts. Orienting students to "lookout for language" (Monahan and Henken 2003) is key to framing an environment where students develop a "language to talk about language" (Derewianka 1990).

Snakes! Accessing Students' Language Resources and Content Schema

In the next example, Kim Gilbert used a mentor text to help students recognize how an author can use a nonfiction format to convey information (Cornerstone Initiative 2008). To achieve this aim, Ms. Gilbert engaged a small group of students in a guided reading of an informational text: *Snakes* by M. Dufresne (2007). To begin, she invited five students to do a "picture walk" as a prereading activity. She first directed their attention to a chart developed during a recent whole-group minilesson (Figure 5.2). This chart exhibited some of the features of informational texts (labels, photographs, captions, tables of contents), and Ms. Gilbert hoped it would prompt the students to unpack how the author of *Snakes* shaped the text to help her readers better understand concepts related to snakes. Ms. Gilbert then guided her students page by page through the book, which was specifically written to expose young children to informational features and thus contained photographs and simple text. It also contained specific features that Ms. Gilbert wanted students to notice, including technical vocabulary such as *reptiles, camouflage, venom, prey,* and *fangs.*

In Figure 5.2 on page 72, we include excerpts from the lesson along with our own commentary on how two struggling writers connected their prior knowledge about the content (snakes) and language as they explored the text.

Figure 5.2   Chart Showing Features of Nonfiction Texts

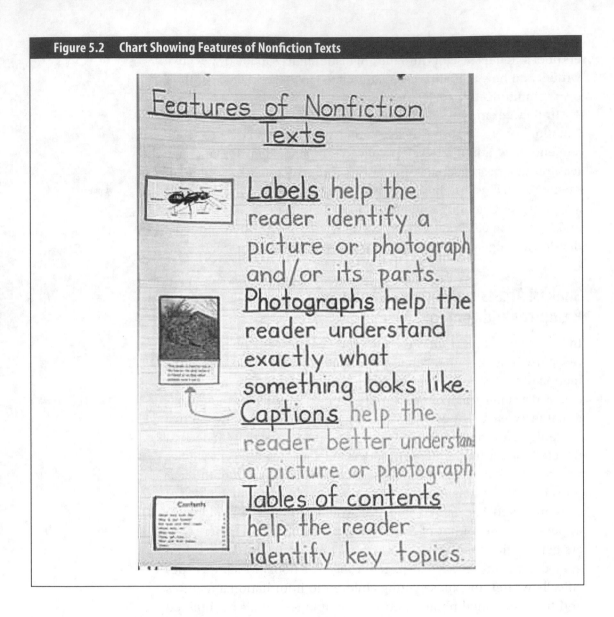

As she talked about language, Ms. Gilbert showed that she valued what students already knew, and she explicitly guided them to connect their knowledge with the concepts in the text. Ms. Gilbert carefully scaffolded terminology and concepts that pointed students to the goals of why they were reading and writing, such as, "Remember, we always read for meaning!" and "Who is the audience?" In this way, she

Ms. Gilbert:	What do you know about snakes?	Ms. Gilbert elicits what students know about the topic—snakes.
Carlos:	I know something. . . . They eats . . . They eat . . . They eat like . . . They eat meat.	
Ms. Gilbert:	They eat meat. OK. What else do you guys know about snakes?	
Ariel:	Some snakes . . . Water snakes eat people.	
Ms. Gilbert:	You think some snakes eat people?	Ms. Gilbert scaffolds student comments into a question. She is positioning the students to *ask* questions of the text, not simply to *respond* to questions about the text.
Ariel:	Um hmm.	
Ms. Gilbert:	Maybe. So that's a question that you have. Excellent, Ariel. *Do* snakes eat people? I don't know. That's a great question. Carlos?	
Carlos:	My mom . . . My dad he . . . he bought a snake. But then it got he . . . he sold it to my uncle, his brother, and . . . and . . . and then it got lost . . . outside.	Ms. Gilbert continues to foreground what students know ("*you* know") and connect this to the concept with language that helps them recognize and connect what they know in order to build meaning with what the author is presenting. She also continues to support students with language
Ms. Gilbert:	Oh my goodness. *You* know something about snakes. You know that some people keep snakes as . . .	
Carlos:	A pet.	
Ms. Gilbert:	Pets.	

Carlos:	One time I saw a guy riding a bike with a *big* yellow, um, snake on his back.	that helps them set authentic purposes by asking questions of an informational text.
Ms. Gilbert:	Oh my goodness. So we got our schema ready. We have one question—Do snakes eat people? Do we have any other questions? Maria?	Not all students are ready to ask questions. Maria *is* making a text connection to her own experience, but she may need further guidance about questioning a text as well as learning the language to do this.
Maria:	Ummm. At my house, right? . . .	
Ms. Gilbert:	Shhh. I want to hear what Maria's question [is] about snakes . . .	
Maria:	My mom's nephew . . . he got a little thing. Right? He told me. I said, "What is the thing for?"	
Ms. Gilbert:	So, some more schema about people keeping snakes as pets.	
Maria:	(*not intelligible*)	
Ms. Gilbert:	Yeah, look at that big snake. Let's open up to the first page. Wow. What do we see here? What do we see? Ariel.	Notice how Kim scaffolds students to *look out for text features*— in this case bold font as a signal for technical vocabulary (*reptile*)!
Ariel:	A snake.	
Ms. Gilbert:	A snake. Now I'm noticing as I look at the text over here, there's one word in darker print than the rest	

	of the words. . . . When a word in a nonfiction book is in dark, bold print like that, it means that it's a very important word. . . . Let's look at the first part, the R-E-P.	
Carlos:	Rep.	
Ms. Gilbert:	Rep. Now let's move on to the next part.	
Carlos:	Ti . . . les . . .	
Ms. Gilbert:	Reptiles. Very good, Carlos. . . . Snakes belong to a group of animals called reptiles.	
Ariel:	Are they . . . ? Do they blend in with stuff?	The student now initiates her question without scaffolding.
Ms. Gilbert:	Do they blend in with things? Do they camouflage? We're gonna have to read . . . We're gonna have to read on to find out. OK, right now we're picture walking though.	
Ms. Gilbert:	What are you noticing on this page, Carlos?	Ms. Gilbert tries to get the students to notice how the verb *slither* communicates how snakes move. She acknowledges what Carlos notices and Ariel's meaning making

Carlos:	He's . . . [Ariel moves her arms to show the snake's movement.]	through body movements to define the term further as they discuss the meaning of the term and connect multiple modes of "knowing" to action and to the printed text. Notice how much the students already know and can do (e.g. classifying animals that move without legs—such as a worm). Notice how the dialogic nature of Ms. Gilbert's lesson orients students' awareness of their current knowledge as they are guided to connect this knowledge to new language and concepts central to the topic.
Ms. Gilbert:	What is he doing? Yeah. [Ms. Gilbert points at Ariel and starts to motion to show slithering.]	
Carlos:	That. . . . [Carlos joins in with the slithering motions.]	
Ms. Gilbert:	What do snakes do?	
Carlos:	They . . . to walk they don't have no legs so they go like that.	
Ms. Gilbert:	Yes.	
Carlos:	They slither.	
Ms. Gilbert:	They *slither.* Listen to that word. *Sli . . . ther:* Doesn't it sound like it looks like? Let's slither.	
Carlos:	Oooh, it says it right here.	
Ariel:	Like a worm.	

Several similar exchanges take place as the group explores the book. During this time, Ms. Gilbert helps Ariel connect her earlier question about "blending in" to the concept and terminology for *camouflage* found on a later page. At the end, Ms. Gilbert summarizes (below).

Ms. Gilbert:	OK, so we have had some of our questions answered just by taking a picture walk. We found out that	Before sending students off to read and discuss the text independently, Ms.

	some snakes *do* camouflage, but we're still wondering about whether or not snakes can eat people. So, I would like you to close up now and you're gonna whisper read. As you're reading, you're gonna notice if you learn something new. OK. I'm gonna come around and listen to your reading.	Gilbert summarizes by reminding them that the purpose of the text is for sharing factual information and that this text type was written to provide answers to satisfy readers' curiosity and interest in snakes as a subspecies of the reptile family. From an early age, students are accessing text types that help them classify and describe.

invited dialogue in which students noticed and contributed their own knowledge about form, function, and meaning of the printed text.

Focusing on How Authors Develop the "Ideas" in Their Texts

In line with the goal of explicitly teaching struggling writers language for reading and writing that is increasingly complex, teachers could also use whole-class or small-group minilessons to draw attention to how authors *explain* and *describe* in scientific texts. Teachers can draw students' attention to the linguistic processes used in the *Snakes* text that explain, describe, or express action (e.g., *slither*). For instance, page 2 contains two sentences:

Snakes are reptiles.
Reptiles are animals that have scales for skin.

The use of the verb "to be" ("Reptiles *are*") enables the author of *Snakes* to explain scientific relationships: Snakes ARE reptiles; reptiles ARE animals. The form of the verb "to have" allows the author to describe characteristics of snakes. For example, the phrase "that have scales for skin" elaborates and adds complexity by providing descriptive characteristics specific to reptiles. Action verbs such as *slither* develop the concept of how snakes and other legless animals move.

Teachers can also encourage students' language awareness by "collecting" and charting words during the study of genre-specific texts. This activity increases the language choices available to students as they learn to think and communicate scientific concepts. Asking students to look at language patterns common to specific genres provides students with the language they will need to represent their ideas when doing their own writing in science (or other academic genres). Some questions to prompt such discussions might include:

- What verbal processes (e.g., "slither") are found?
- Who or what are the participants (often technical nouns or noun phrases)?
- What are the circumstances (prepositional phrases that answer questions about how a process occurs, why is occurs, or how long it took)?

Such focus in analyzing language provides students with practice in locating meaning, discussing meanings, and looking at language patterns common to specific genres. Charting provides students' access to such language for future writing events.

Focusing on How Authors Use Language to Create Particular Relationships Between Text and Readers

The purpose of informational texts such as *Snakes* is to create an exchange of information between authors and readers. Adjectives and adverbial clauses use factual language that describes and explains. Declarative statements deliver information directly with little evaluation or appraisal. For example, on page 10 of *Snakes,* the author makes the following points (underlines added):

> *Some snakes have venom.*
> *They kill their prey with venom.*
> *The snake bites into its prey with <u>big</u> teeth called fangs.*
> *Then the venom goes into the prey and kills it.*

Getting early readers to notice phrases such as "big teeth" that help describe and explain (define) how snakes deliver venom to their prey prepares students to begin working with increasingly complex and abstract ideas in their own writing.

Focusing on the Structural Features that Create a Coherent, Whole Text

Ms. Gilbert's lesson focused primarily on how authors of informational texts construct texts *as a whole* to ask questions and provide answers that are easy for readers to locate. Becoming familiar with the bold typeface of technical vocabulary and with the glossary prepares young readers to scan for headings and subheadings, use an index, and peruse graphics with captions as they seek information. Ms. Gilbert's chart identified the features the class explored in other informational texts, which also included tables of contents, diagrams, and labels.

Ms. Gilbert could have also used the *Snakes* text to draw her students' attention to the ways intratextual features can be used to create coherent texts. Consider the following excerpts from the *Snakes* text (underlines added):

> <u>Some snakes</u> have venom.
> <u>They</u> kill their prey with venom.
> <u>The snake</u> bites into its prey with big teeth called fangs.
> <u>Then</u> the venom goes into the prey and kills it.

Pointing out how the author foregrounds the topic as she begins each sentence (*some snakes, the snake, they*) could draw students' attention to how the author makes language choices that focus and develop her ideas throughout the text. Helping students track topic-pronoun relationships within the text (*snakes = they*) or the use of connectors such as *then* develops their awareness of how the author builds connected sequences. As young readers work with scientific texts, they see how patterns are used across specific texts and begin to learn how to use them to construct coherent and comprehensible ideas in their own writing.

"Writing a Garden": Writing Multiple Genres to Learn Science Content

This section explores how Mary Moran guided her third-grade students to write using multiple genres during a thematic unit to see reading-writing connections in action. Ms. Moran's reading and writing workshop focused on thematic units in history and science, with the goal of engaging a diverse group of urban third graders in academic content relevant to their lives that would contribute to their school success. Each morning, Ms. Moran's students gathered on the rug where she read a "mentor" text aloud. During and after reading, she guided a group discussion of these texts explicitly focusing on different aspects of the language used and the themes conveyed. Over the course of a school year, Ms. Moran's students studied several thematic units and chose multi-genre texts connected to these topics, which included: famous Americans, the abolitionist movement, and the science of gardening and food production.

Ms. Moran felt strongly that all students, regardless of their reading and writing abilities, needed exposure to complex texts through scaffolded discussions as well as opportunities to explore texts independently and with peers. In addition to the leveled books used for skill instruction, Ms. Moran's students explored a range of fiction; nonfiction; poetry; adult picture books, such as *The Middle Passage* by Tom Feelings (1995) and *Hungry Planet: What the World Eats* by Peter Menzel and Faith D'Aluisio (2007); and everyday texts, such as seed packets and recipes. Ms. Moran kept a list of these texts on the wall. On May 15, Ms. Moran's class discussed *From Seed to Plant* (Gibbons 1993) and headed to the raised garden bed they had created outdoors from materials donated by the city's food bank.

Having already planted lettuce and kale, their "text" for the day was a packet of carrot seeds that Patrick had brought from home. Ms. Moran shared photocopies of both sides of the seed packet with her students, and a lively discussion ensued as the children examined the information and directions. A week earlier, Ms. Moran had exposed her students to some of the procedural language on the lettuce packet. Now they considered imperative verbs written in bold capital letters, such as **SOW** and **KEEP MOIST.** One student noticed a phrase: "**SOAK** seeds for six hours before planting." They realized that they needed to implement this step before planting.

A Classroom Teacher's Guide to Struggling Writers

Ms. Moran asked the students how this verb differed from what the lettuce packet had advised. The students remembered that the lettuce packet asked them to "**KEEP SEEDS EVENLY MOIST.**" In the discussion that ensued, one student commented that the verb *water* was too general; thus, more specific vocabulary, such as *soak* and *moisten,* was needed for different purposes. "If you soaked the lettuce seeds with a hose, they would wash away," one student explained. Through "language in use," students were building a lexicon of specific language processes to fit specific communication needs.

Mrs. Moran then redirected the students' attention to the text on the carrot seed packet. Together, they identified that it was broken into three sections:

1. *The story of the carrot:* Orange is a relatively new color for carrots. The original carrots from Afghanistan were purple, red, or white, which is the color of wild carrots found in North America. Yellow carrots were grown in Turkey by the tenth century, orange ones were developed later by the Dutch, and the French continued breeding new varieties.

2. *The description of the carrot variety:* An heirloom French carrot that does well for most gardeners. Sweet and tasty at any size; free from hard fiber. Best for eating fresh from the garden.

3. *Procedures or hints:* GARDEN HINT: Soil should be loose, rich, and rock free to a depth of at least 6″ to 9″ for well-grown, full-size carrots. Soak seeds for 6 hours before sowing. Wait for a couple of cold snaps before fall harvests, as the cold weather makes many carrots sweeter.

The discussion shifted as students made connections between the text on the packet and previous units they had studied earlier in the year. For example, one student, reading that yellow carrots originated in Turkey, recalled their study of the freed slave and abolitionist Olaudah Equiano. The student noted, "Slave ships often stopped in Turkey." Later, he and a friend located Turkey on the world map.

"What does *heirloom* mean?" asked another student, noticing the term on the packet. Ms. Moran and the class then talked about the heirloom seeds the class had gathered at a local historical site during their recent study of famous Americans. A third student read further and commented that she had never seen purple, red, or white carrots.

Discussions like these clearly show the children's engagement in their learning. They stem from Ms. Moran's ongoing commitment to provide students with opportunities to develop the conventions of group discussion, to learn to pose useful questions, and to use language to build concepts through social exchanges around texts. Over time, students also began to draw on these emerging skills in their writing.

Linking Text Analysis to Writing for Specific Purposes and Audiences

Like many teachers in large, urban school districts, Ms. Moran is accountable for demonstrating that her students have learned the scope and sequence of skills in the basal reading series and the high-stakes state reading literacy test. And, like other teachers in her district, Ms. Moran is required to occasionally assess her students' writing using the kinds of prompts they could expect to encounter on the high-stakes tests. Composition prompts usually require students to recount an experience. Recounts include "narrating a sequence of events and communicating their significance to an audience" (Schleppegrell and Go 2007, 530). So when asked to recount his first days of planting, Kobe created this entry in his writing notebook (Figure 5.3), Mrs. Moran noticed that he included the following key features:

- An introductory sentence.
- A list of vegetables planted.
- Some colorful language, which invites the reader to read more.
- A mention of three garden tools.
- A definition of one of the tools he used.

At the same time, she noted that although his entry included lots of detail, it still needed more focus, cohesion, and depth.

Struggling writers like Kobe often need practice distinguishing language features, such as language that would help him recount an

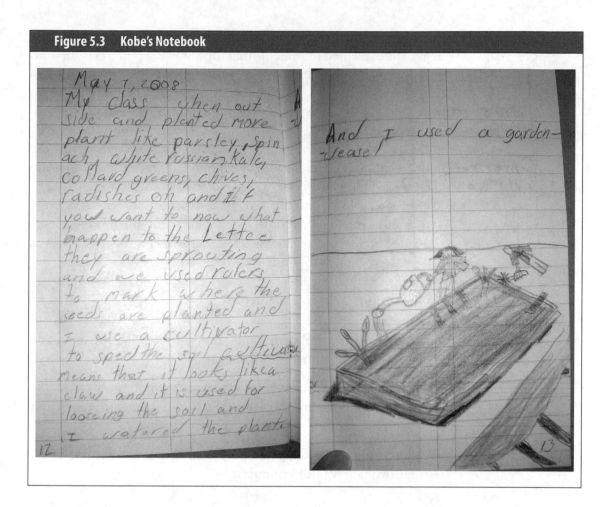

Figure 5.3 Kobe's Notebook

May 7, 2008
My class when out side and planted more plant like parsley, spinach, white russian kale, collard greens, chives, radishes oh and if you want to now what happen to the Lettce they are sprouting and we used rulers to mark where the seeds are planted and I use a cultivator to sped the soil cultivator means that it looks like a claw and it is used for loosing the soil and I watered the plant

12

And I used a garden-weasel

13

experience, language that would help him define procedures, and language that would engage or invite a reader to read further. They also need a better sense of when and how to use such language features to organize a coherent text. As Ms. Moran identified, Kobe needed to learn how to make choices and control those features for deeper meaning making (for example, "showing significance")—not only to increase his chances for success when he must write a recount for test purposes but, more important, also to provide him with tools for learning new and complex concepts.

Ms. Moran decided to create a writing task connected to the students' garden work that would prepare Kobe and her other students for the particular demands of a high-stakes writing assessment. To begin, she explained to students that the following year's class of third graders would inherit the garden. Next, she asked them what kind of text might help the new gardeners understand how to keep the garden going. Based on their exploration of mentor texts throughout the year, the students had many suggestions, but they finally decided to write individual books that followed a similar format. They agreed that the books would each contain a table of contents, an introduction to invite the reader into the book, a "how to plant" section, and a glossary. As they had explored and enjoyed books of poetry, students suggested adding individual poems to the book. Finally, wishing to encourage students' choice and ownership, Mary also asked them to create a self-selected piece at the end.

As they drafted each section, Ms. Moran divided the writing workshop into three daily time segments:

- "Rug time" for whole-group planning and for charting ideas and language (approximately ten minutes).

- Quiet time, which students used to work on drafts and Ms. Moran used to hold conferences with selected students (approximately fifteen minutes).

- Sharing time, which involved peer sharing or whole-group sharing (approximately fifteen minutes).

During rug time, Ms. Moran's students discussed the purpose of creating a good introduction for their audience of new third graders who, like most of them before this year, had never gardened. They created a chart listing these purposes, which included "to help people learn how to garden"; "to explain how seeds germinate"; and "if you have never gardened, this is a guide book."

The students then worked on their drafts of their introductions for ten minutes during quiet time. During conferences and check-ins, Ms. Moran noticed some students "got it," but she also realized that, although the class had set the purpose and audience for the book, some children needed more scaffolding to understand that an introduction must include language to "hook" the readers to want to read further, as well as to preview what was to come. Some students had also experienced "genre confusion" (Gebhard, Harman, and Seger 2007) and started right in with a how-to paragraph.

At the conclusion of quiet time, Ms. Moran asked if any students wished to share. Listening to and discussing each other's work in the whole group provided additional support for students who were struggling. Here is Tiana's piece:

> Hi, my name is Tiana and I'm writing this book to help you grow a garden. In these chapters you will learn about what tools you need, how deep you need to plant them, and how to keep them alive. I hope I answered all your questions and I hope you have all the information you need about gardening. "enjoy"

As volunteers read aloud, Ms. Moran facilitated a discussion about which language choices were most effective for inviting the readers to enter the book. For example, Tiana introduced herself as a helper and invited them to enjoy the book. Her classmates agreed that using the word *enjoy* was a very effective way to welcome readers and invite them to continue with the text. Ms. Moran also pointed out that Tiana personalized the text through a *thinking/feeling* process ("you will learn"). Furthermore, Tiana included a complex sentence that succinctly previewed multiple clauses to foreshadow what the reader would learn: *what tools, how deep,* and *how to keep the garden alive.*

After Tiana read her piece, several students went back to revise what they had written by adding text to their own introductions. Tim, for example, had originally used verbs such as *dig down, plant,* and *harvest* in his introduction. But during sharing time, he quickly realized that this procedural language was not the best choice for an effective introduction. He explained to the class, "I think I need to save my writing for the next chapter that tells how to plant." The next day, Tim was a vocal participant as the class charted the "how to" section.

The following day, Ms. Moran used a chart to help students with procedural verbs, such as *soak, dig down, separate,* and *space.* She then conducted a brief minilesson on connectors, which she explained help create cohesiveness in "how to" texts that involve a step-by-step process (Figure 5.4).

Figure 5.4   "How To" Language

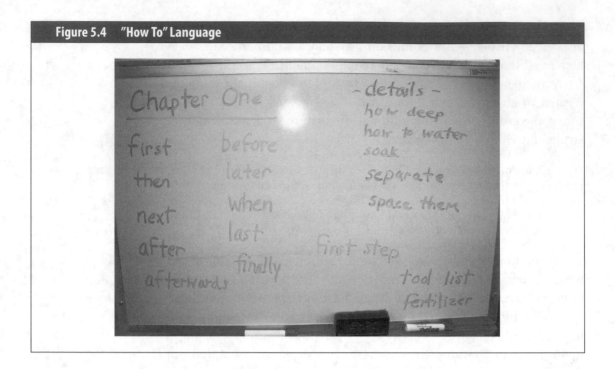

Summary

Both Ms. Gilbert and Ms. Moran teach young children in large culturally, linguistically, and economically diverse urban school districts. Both classrooms included struggling writers, some of whom were English language learners. Orienting their students as critical and social "language detectives" (Monahan and Henken 2003) Ms. Gilbert and Ms. Moran structured their teaching to create an environment where students learned language by using language. They were careful to make sure that even struggling students had access to complex texts and were not denied access to rich ideas for learning content. But they didn't assume that because students had been exposed to new language in class, they were ready to independently make the language choices they needed as academic writers. Such assumptions *create* struggling students through lack of responsive teaching. Instead, Ms. Gilbert and Ms. Moran continually monitored and structured lessons that explicitly helped each student develop as a writer. See additional resources for teaching students about the language choices effective writers make below.

Resources for Teaching and Assessing Writing with a Genre-Specific Focus

Annandale, K., R. Bindon, J. Broz, J. Dougan, K. Handley, A. Johnston, L. Lockett, P. Lynch, and R. Rourke. 2006. *First Steps Second Edition: Writing Resource Book*. Beverly, MA: STEPS Professional Development.

Derewianka, B. 1990. *Exploring How Texts Work*. Australia: Primary English Teaching Association.

Gebhard, M., R. Harman, and W. Seger. 2007. "Reclaiming Recess: Learning the Language of Persuasion." *Language Arts* 84 (5): 419–30.

Knapp, P., and Watkins, M. 2005. *Genre, Text, Grammar: Technologies for Teaching and Assessing Writing*. Sydney, Australia: University of South Wales Press.

Schleppegrell, M. 2007. *The Language of Schooling: A Functional Linguistics Perspective*. Mahwah, NJ: Lawrence Erlbaum Publishers.

Schleppegrell, M. J., and A. L. Go. 2007. "Analyzing the Writing of English Learners: A Functional Approach." *Language Arts* 84: 529–38.

6

Assessments that Promote Effective and Purposeful Writing

The key to providing appropriate support and direction for struggling writers is careful, ongoing assessment focused on students' ability to fulfill their communicative intentions with various audiences in particular social contexts. Whereas traditional assessment focuses on standards of correctness in student writing, we ask a very different set of questions:

- *What* is the student doing when she writes?
- Does the writing *work*?
- If not, why doesn't it work, and what does the student need to learn to write more effectively?
- What kind of instruction is needed, and what should teachers' instructional priorities be?
- What skill or strategy should teachers focus on first?

In this chapter we do not present a compendium of assessment practices. Instead, we present illustrations of how teachers examine the effectiveness of children's writing for the purpose of planning appropriate instruction.

In Chapter 4, we illustrated what effective teachers of writing do when they plan and execute writing conferences with students. We begin this chapter with an example of a kindergarten teacher who used a process called *descriptive review* (Carini and Himley 2000) to evaluate what an emergent writer already knew about writing for a specific purpose. Then we examine writing rubrics and discuss how teachers use specific linguistic information to address specific writing forms and functions.

Introducing Kyra

Kyra was a kindergarten student in an elementary school of approximately nine hundred students in a large urban district. She spoke Spanish at home, but she used English proficiently in classroom activities. Her teacher, Jane Dement, was interested in examining Kyra's writing to see *what she already knew* when she wrote for a particular purpose—in this case, as Kyra wrote in her journal to connect to a variety of literature Ms. Dement read aloud each day.

Ms. Dement worried that writing assessments for young students tended to focus narrowly on the accuracy of print conventions, such as spelling or sentence structure. Although Kyra's knowledge in this area was important, especially in light of her background with multiple languages, Ms. Dement wanted a fuller picture of how Kyra was expressing herself through her writing. Therefore, she realized that it was important to consider multiple dimensions about Kyra as a student writer, such as Kyra's success as a *composer* of ideas, an *editor* who understands structures and conventions, and an *author* who understands that her writing has power. Figure 6.1 discusses these different dimensions further.

Ms. Dement was committed to providing literacy instruction that addressed the "basic skills" of reading and writing as outlined in the district's standardized curriculum, but she also valued the linguistic and cultural knowledge her students brought to their learning. Therefore, Ms. Dement's kindergarten literacy block included multiple experiences with children's literature and other activities that encouraged children to personally connect to their reading and

Figure 6.1	Dimensions of Student as Writer

Student as Composer

Young writers are often able to compose complex texts orally or with other media, such as drawing, before they can actually write them down (King and Rentell 1979; Harste, Woodward, and Burke 1984; Donovan and Smolkin 2002; Wilson 2002). Attending to what students know about composing ideas is especially important for teachers of students who are emergent writers as well as students learning literacy when English is an additional language.

Student as Editor

Young writers need to understand how form or structure contributes to effective communication of the intended message. This includes understanding editorial conventions such as text organization, spelling, syntax, and punctuation (Bearne 2002; Wilson 2002). It is important to identify students who think of writing as *only* an editorial process. These students are often overly concerned with correct spelling and are fearful of making mistakes. As a result, they compose little on initial drafts (Wilson 2002).

Student as Author

Young writers are building a sense of themselves as authors. That is, they are developing an understanding of themselves as literate participants in their world (Luke and Freebody 1997; Wilson 2002). This includes realizing that they can control language for their own purposes and goals both academically *and* socially. This involves learning enough about language to make their own *meaningful* choices as writers (Brannon and Knoblauch 1984; Derewianka 1990).

Adapted from Wilson 2002

writing. For instance, she asked her kindergarteners to draw and write every day in a journal to encourage them to connect to and extend their responses to daily read-aloud literature. Sometimes she provided prompts, such as, "Can you write about a time when you were scared?" in the hope that journal writing would encourage her students to connect a read-aloud theme to their own lives. At other times, she encouraged students to respond more generally to a book they'd read and discussed in class.

A Classroom Teacher's Guide to Struggling Writers

Kyra's journal contained fiction and nonfiction themes for which she used drawings and emergent writing. There were several pages with drawings of animals (worms, whales, birds), for example, and simple statements such as "the waool can swam" (*The whale can swim*). Other pages included text-to-life connections, such as, "I wass sardr wdd I wass a btab and I ssa a sree snow mnn" (*I was scared when I was a baby and I saw a scary snowman*).

Ms. Dement used journal writing for both instruction and assessment. Kyra's journal, for example, contained a wealth of data demonstrating Kyra's emerging composition, editorial, and authorial knowledge. Her journals also provided Ms. Dement with data for longitudinal assessment as the complexity of her printed texts—ranging from simple, one-sentence entries to more complex entries—could be tracked over time and by topic. The piece of Kyra's writing focused on here is presented in Figure 6.2. This entry responded to a series of books in the *Elmer Series* by David McKee that Ms. Dement had read to the class. This series revolves around the adventures of an elephant named Elmer, who has a multicolored patchwork hide.

Assessing Kyra's Writing

Ms. Dement worked with several of her colleagues to assess Kyra's writing, using a process called *descriptive review* (Carini and Himley 2000), which involves two or more people who look at the same piece of work, describe what they notice, and, sometimes, share recommendations for future instruction. In this particular case, Ms. Dement was interested in working with the review group to notice the features present in Kyra's writing and then use these observations to explore how the read-aloud sessions and journal responses were affecting Kyra's growth as an emergent writer.

Before the group met, Ms. Dement reflected on what she wished to learn from the descriptive review process and how best to use the set of observations and writing samples she had collected in Kyra's writing folder. Then, as the group prepared to begin, Ms. Dement identified her question: "What does Kyra already know about written language, and how is she using this knowledge in her journal writing?"

Next, Ms. Dement shared her collection of observations and writing samples, and explained her reason for choosing the Elmer text from Kyra's journal for close analysis. (This text was interesting to

Figure 6.2   Kyra's Writing

Ms. Dement because in it Kyra had begun to include multiple ideas and more complex structures in her printed language.) The group spent some time examining Kyra's colorful text, and then everyone described what they noticed (see Figure 6.3). Importantly, throughout the process, the group oriented its focus directly on features of Kyra's text (e.g., the details in her drawing or her use of capital letters for names) rather than labeling her work (e.g., as "emergent writing" or "on grade level").

Figure 6.3   Notes from Descriptive Review of Kyra's "Elmer" text

Descriptive Review of Student Writing

Child/Group: Kyra, Kindergarten, language background Spanish and English

Context and Goal: Individual journal responses to daily whole-class read aloud and book discussions. Focus text ("Elmer") chosen from several journal entries that included both fiction and nonfiction responses. In this text, Kyra's emergent writing includes a sentence containing multiple clauses. Kyra's teacher wonders how to structure minilessons as well as how to focus Kyra's writing conferences. Kyra has demonstrated enthusiasm in her topics through patient and detailed illustrations. Her teacher wishes to support this enthusiasm for thinking about what she is reading through the mode of writing.

Evidence/Artifacts: A set of journal responses (drawn and written) to both fiction and nonfiction read-alouds. Focus text is response to a book from the "Elmer" series.

Observations in Categories:

A. Student as Composer
   a. Picture closely matches the book
   b. Sentence describes the picture (one depends on the other)
   c. Tone is set with sun smiling down on flower, colorful and vivid artwork, multiple colors
   d. Cohesion expressed through the scene (subject is located under sun, on grass, near tree)
   e. Lots of information conveyed through the detailed drawings: apples, tree, water from trunk, tail raised
   f. Written text tells a story

B. Student as Editor
   a. Spaces between words
   b. Words fit around the picture
   c. Conventions for writing followed: top/down, left/right
   d. Experimenting with letter-sound relationships (e.g., *Aamer* for *Elmer, hees* for *his*)
   e. Letters for beginning sounds in words reflect conventional spelling
   f. 6/8 words represent conventional ending sounds (e.g., Kyra used *t* to correctly represent what she heard in an *-ed* ending)

g. Conventional English syntax, used the connector *and* between two complete clauses

h. Use of double letters (*aa, rr, dd, ll*)

i. Use of uppercase letter to begin the sentence (and a name) and lowercase letters within the sentence

j. Use of past tense

C. Student as Author

a. Careful attention to detail and color in her illustrations (reflects patience and pride in her composition)

b. Willingness to take risks (experimenting with matching letter patterns and sounds from her experience—possibly in both English and Spanish)

c. Draws on multiple resources (spoken language, vocabulary from read-aloud texts—e.g., *swirled, splashed*, details from illustrations in read-aloud picture book)

d. Linked illustrations with text to communicate her ideas

Thoughts and Impressions:

A. What Kyra knows and can do:

As an author, Kyra is enthusiastic. The detail and depth of her journal responses indicate ownership and willingness to spend time as a writer. Responding to read-alouds as mentor texts through the journal activities allows her to scaffold her emerging knowledge of print with her more sophisticated abilities as an artist. She is clearly willing to experiment with connecting her spoken language as well as new language encountered from environmental texts to conventions for spelling and grammar, and she is successfully applying form and structure, including writing a complex sentence with rich vocabulary.

B. Questions and suggestions for further assessment:

a. Do the double letters she included in some spellings reflect her pronunciation and/or experience with Spanish? If so, valuing both languages through contrastive minilessons may further encourage her to code switch and can value her metacognitive literacy awareness in both languages.

b. What growth does this text demonstrate if we looked at her writing from earlier in the year? What growth would this text demonstrate if we looked at several other texts written during the same period of time? If we return to study several more texts from her journal, is there a pattern in her use of more complex sentences across the year or dependent on the topic? For example, does she "tell a story" in some texts but just state a fact in another? Have the print conventions changed across time?

c. If we do a "think-aloud" with Kyra about her writing as part of a conference, what more might she offer about this piece verbally? What questions might be used during a conference to help her link her explanation with new written language?

Actions or Next Steps:

A. Use think aloud technique as a conference protocol. Kyra draws on her resources, both art and written, so teacher can ask her verbally to expand on her ideas and link them to written text.

B. Continue to use "mentor" text read-aloud as daily routine, develop minilessons to focus on elaborating and organizing her texts, work with simple story grammar or descriptive writing on nonfiction topics. For class, continue to focus on illustrations as source of vocabulary, create and post charts of technical or descriptive vocabulary from reading.

Format adapted from: Carini and Himley (2000); Marten and Spielman (2005); Wilson (2002)

In the following sections, we focus on two areas, evidence of Kyra's connections between her emergent writing and her spoken language, as well as her extensive and detailed drawings. We analyze these and offer suggestions helpful in planning next steps for teaching Kyra.

The Role of Dual Languages

The group noted several aspects of Kyra's piece, including her developing mastery of print conventions (student as editor). This included using spaces between her words; writing from left to right; choosing letters for beginning sounds in words that reflect conventional spelling; and using complete simple sentences with capital letters to start. The group also noted that Kyra was experimenting with vowel sounds at the initial and medial positions in words. Remembering that Kyra's home language was Spanish, they also noted her spelling of *his* as *hees,* wondering if this reflected her spoken language, as well as her use of double letters (*rr, ll*) in several words. Ms. Dement resolved to learn more about Kyra's emerging literacy in Spanish as well as English and think of lessons that might build on Kyra's dual languages as a resource.

The Connection Between Literacy and Drawing

The group also noted the rich details in Kyra's drawing. They discussed her persistence, her use of imagination, and the rich thinking these demonstrated. This provided Ms. Dement with an assessment of Kyra's writing that helped her support Kyra's individual development within the routines of the daily literacy block. Based on what she learned through the review, Ms. Dement planned a minilesson for her class on connecting the details in students' drawings to encourage the use of rich vocabulary and adding additional details to simple sentences (*student as composer*).

Developing Criteria for Assessing Students' Writing with Rubrics

In this section we return to third-grader Kobe's garden journal entry to illustrate what the language features needed for recounting his gardening experience are and how they might be assessed using a rubric. To do this we explain why Ms. Moran placed a significant focus on recounting experience. Then, we discuss the language features of personal experience recounts and how these features are affected by writers' purposes, audiences, and the social context. Finally, we share a rubric for assessing what Kobe knows about the language needed for writing a recount and we discuss how Ms. Moran could use this rubric to determine what additional support he needs in order to write more effectively. Rubrics are another useful tool for providing teachers with the data they need in order to offer explicit support and direction for struggling writers.

The Importance of Recounting Experience

In her third-grade classroom, Ms. Moran placed a significant focus of her writing program on recounting experience. She recognized that personal experience recounts are narratives that enable her students to build on their background knowledge and experience. Students are also highly motivated by the social connections they make as they share this kind of writing with their peers (Dyson 1993). Furthermore, students' ability to recount personal experiences is assessed on the Massachusetts Comprehensive Assessment System, grade four writing prompt. Students spend extensive time in third grade preparing for this test. Here is the prompt for the 2007 writing assessment:

> Think about the best time that you have ever had. Maybe you played all day with friends outside, went on a special trip, participated in a game, or spent some time at camp. Write a story about this best time. What were you doing? Who was with you? Where were you? Why was this the best time ever? Give enough details in the story to show the reader what happened. (Massachusetts Department of Elementary and Secondary Education 2007, online)

Ms. Moran also realized that she could build on personal experience recounts to help her students learn more academic writing genres, such as reporting on science experiments or recounting historical events (Schleppegrell and Go 2007). Learning to notice the language features of personal experience recounts helped Ms. Moran's students to begin discussing the differences between fictional "stories" and nonfictional accounts of what happened in their own lives. Recount narratives also connected readily to the third-grade history curriculum, including, for example, units focusing on famous Americans and the Abolition Movement, as these involved recounts of the lives of others.

Constructing a Rubric for a Recount of Personal Experience

After Ms. Moran's students worked in the class garden, she usually asked them to write about what they'd accomplished that day and then share their experiences with their classmates. Here is an excerpt from Kobe's journal (also see Figure 5.3) that recounted his experience in the garden.

> My class when out side and planted more plant like parsley, spin-ach, white Russian Kale, collard greens, chives, radishes oh and if you want to now what happen to the Lettce they are sprouting and we used

rulers to mark where the seeds are planed and I use a cultivator to sped the soil cultivates means that it looks like a claw and it is used for looseing the soil and I watered the plants. And I used a garden-weasel.

Fundamentally, personal experience recounts require language that "tells what happened." The rubric presented in the next section assesses how well Kobe's journal entry *tells what happened in the garden*. The criteria for the grading rubric presented here are adapted from Annandale et al. (2006), Derewianka (1990), and Schleppegrell and Go (2007).

Criteria for Personal Recount

Purpose: To tell what happened

Type of writing: Personal recount—retelling of an activity that the writer has personally experienced. (Other recount types might include a *factual recount* that records the particulars of an incident or an *imaginative recount* in which the writer takes an imaginary role and gives details of events.)

Content: What was it about? What is the purpose for writing this? Who is the audience? Conveys a real experience to an audience either present (e.g., reading to classmates) or distant (e.g., a letter to parents or an article for the school newspaper).

Text Organization (Structure and Coherence):

   a. Orientation: Introduces the background information the reader needs to understand the text (who, what, where, when, what happened?)

   b. Series of events ordered in chronological sequence (e.g., first, second, next, last)

   c. Ending reflection or personal comment throughout (writer shares own ideas/thoughts/analysis beyond factual retelling)

Language Features:

Names specific participants (people, animals, objects)

Uses simple past tense

Uses mostly action verbs (doing, saying, showing)

Uses linking items (connectors) that show time, sequence, and location (*first, next, later, then, on, in*)

Details are relevant to purpose

For personal recount uses first-person pronouns (*I, we*)

Provides cohesion by clear linking between pronouns and referents (classmates = they)

Using these criteria we constructed a rubric (adding conventions such as spelling and punctuation) specific to Kobe's and his class-mates' journal writing but also useful for other writing where recount is utilized (Figure 6.4).

Applying this rubric to Kobe's text (Figure 6.5), we note, for example, that he provided a simplistic orientation that included an intro-ductory sentence; a list of vegetables planted; some colorful language inviting the reader to read more; and mention of three garden tools with a more elaborated definition of one of the tools and how he used it. His entry included lots of details, but it needed more focus, cohesion, and depth. Kobe included many of the language features that explain "what happened," but he did not organize them sequentially into a coherent text. He primarily used *and* to connect his events rather than time/sequence connectors such as *first, then, next, or finally.*

After assessing this text and others written by her students, Ms. Moran noticed that several of the writers did not sequence their key events. In response, she developed a minilesson for the class on how to use linking terms that show time sequence (see Figure 5.4). Other minilessons might have included focusing on how to write an in-troduction that orients or "sets the stage" for the recount. During a teacher-student conference with Kobe, Ms. Moran might have com-plimented him on his inclusion of unit vocabulary (such as identify-ing the garden tools he used) and on his decision to elaborate by de-scribing and explaining the purpose of using certain tools, such as the cultivator. She also could have asked him to read his piece and fo-cus on how to recognize and divide clauses into sentences marked by correct punctuation. As another option, she could have encour-aged Kobe to add language that included his own perspective on the events.

It is important for teachers to show students that writing involves making choices as part of the process of deeper meaning making (for example, "showing significance"). As Kobe continued to revise this recount and wrote new ones, he not only learned the features of writing a recount for the test purposes but, more important, he learned language tools for thinking and writing about new and com-plex concepts.

Figure 6.4 Rubric for Recounting a Personal Experience

Purpose: Recount or tell *what happened*

Type of Recount (circle one): Personal, Factual, Imaginative

Criteria for a Writing a Recount	Evidence of Criteria in Student Writing	Score		
		3	2	1
Content and Purpose: **3:** Chooses format and vocabulary specifically suited to *showing or telling a particular audience* of readers *what happened* (e.g., sharing with classmates, letter to parents or friends, article in school newspaper). **2:** Uses a partial organizational framework *to show or tell what happened* but may mix formats and focus in a way that is not cohesive (e.g., inappropriately mixes a procedural account [*how to do*] with a retelling of events [*what we did*]).				

Adapted from Annandale et al. (2004); Derewianka (1990); and Schleppegrell and Go (2007)

		3	2	1

1: Provides simplistic retelling of experience for undefined audience or includes unclear sequence of events.

Text Organization (Structure and Coherence)

	3	2	1
Orientation:			

Orientation:

3: Language sets the scene and aims to interest the reader (vivid contextual and environmental details that impact the events that unfold).

2: Sufficient information to provide context (details about who, when, where, what, why, how).

1: Few or simplistic details that help the reader understand the setting or context in which the events happened (e.g., may tell who and where but not when).

Series of Events:

3: Includes significant events in chronological order and consistently elaborates on those events so that the reader can visualize the experience. Chooses to include dialogue or quoted speech for impact.

2: Includes events in chronological order with some elaboration about participants that affect the events. Some use of dialogue or reported speech to *show* not just tell about the experience.

1: Includes some events in sequence.

Figure 6.4 *(continued)*

Criteria for a Writing a Recount	Evidence of Criteria in Student Writing	Score		
		3	2	1
Conclusion or Reflection: **3:** Concludes with personal reflection, makes evaluative comments, or summarizes the event (or includes personal comments throughout). **2:** Shares own ideas/thoughts/analysis beyond factual retelling somewhere in the text. **1:** No personal comments or very general (e.g., "It was fun!")				

Specific Language Features of a Recount	Evidence of Language Features in Student Writing	Score Below		
		3	2	1
Specific Language Features of a Recount: **3:** Consistent and innovative **2:** Correct and consistent **1:** Simple (little variety) or inconsistent				
Includes specific participants, such as people, animals, objects.				

Uses simple past tense (e.g., *we walked, they sang, the ducks waddled*).			
Uses mostly action verbs (e.g., doing, saying, showing verbs such as *painted, called, drenched*).			
Includes linking items that show time, sequence, and location (e.g., *first, next, later, then, on, in*).			
Details are relevant to purpose.			
For personal recount, uses first-person pronouns (*I, we*).			
Includes clear linking between pronouns and referents (classmates = they) that provide cohesion.			
Includes conventions of spelling and punctuation.			

Figure 6.5   Assessing Kobe's Text

My class when out side and planted more plant like parsley, spin-ach, white Russian Kale, collard greens, chives, radishes oh and if you want to now what happen to the Lettce they are sprouting and we used rulers to mark where the seeds are planed and I use a cultivator to sped the soil cultivates means that it looks like a claw and it is used for looseing the soil and I watered the plants. And I used a garden-weasel.

Purpose: Recount or tell *what happened*

Type of Recount (circle one): (Personal), Factual, Imaginative

Criteria	Evidence of Criteria in Student Writing	Score		
		3	2	1
Content and Purpose: **3:** Chooses format and vocabulary specifically suited to *showing or telling a particular audience* of readers *what happened* (e.g., sharing with classmates, letter to parents or friends, article in school newspaper). **2:** Uses a partial organizational framework *to show or tell what happened* but may mix formats and focus in a way that is not cohesive (e.g., inappropriately mixes a procedural account [*how to do*] with a retelling of events [*what we did*]).	Language "oh and if you want to now (know) what happened" invites the reader to share Kobe's excitement about making a garden. He is oriented to an audience and he demonstrates his intention to share information with his readers about what is happening in the garden and what he and his class-mates did to create it. He mixes language that recounts "what happened" ("I used a cultivator to sped [spread] the soil") with definitions (e.g., "cultivates means that it looks		x	

		3	2	1

like a claw") and explanations about garden tools and their uses ("it is used for looseing [loosening] the soil"). His mixing of these language features shows that he is ready to elaborate but is not yet consistent about doing this across the text or any particular sequence.

1: Provides simplistic retelling of experience for undefined audience or includes unclear sequence of events.

Text Organization (Structure and Coherence)

Criteria	3	2	1
Orients with a simple introductory sentence that tells who, what, where. Does not explain "outside" or provide any language that focuses or helps the reader imagine the setting: where the garden is located or where in time this event occurred ("planted more plant [plants]" and "the Lettce [lettuce] they are sprouting" infers that this is a moment in time—that the garden was started earlier).			x

Orientation:

3: Language sets the scene and aims to interest the reader (vivid contextual and environmental details that impact the events that unfold).

2: Sufficient information to provide context (details about who, when, where, what, why, how).

1: Few or simplistic details that help the reader understand the setting or context in which the events happened (e.g., may tell who and where but not when).

Figure 6.5 (*continued*)

Criteria	Evidence of Criteria in Student Writing	Score		
		3	2	1
Series of Events: **3:** Includes significant events in chronological order and consistently elaborates on those events so that the reader can visualize the experience. Chooses to include dialogue or quoted speech for impact. **2:** Includes events in chronological order with some elaboration about participants that affect the events. Some use of dialogue or reported speech to *show* not just tell about the experience. **1:** Includes some events in sequence.	Includes significant events: planting, measuring, cultivating, watering. Attempts to elaborate or "show" with descriptive language ("and I use a cultivator to sped the soil cultivates means that it looks like a claw and it is used for looseing the soil") and some complex clause structures ("we used rulers to mark where the seeds are planted"; "if you want to know what happened to the Lettce they are sprouting"). Events not clearly sequenced over time (first, next, last . . .).			x

	3	2	1
Conclusion or Reflection: 3: Concludes with personal reflection, makes evaluative comments, or summarizes the event (or includes personal comments throughout). 2: Shares own ideas/thoughts/analysis beyond factual retelling somewhere in the text. 1: No personal comments or very general (e.g., "It was fun!")	Language is enthusiastic but there is no text that includes his own reflection or personal comments.		x

	3	2	1
Language Features: 3: Consistent and innovative 2: Correct and consistent 1: Simple (little variety) or inconsistent	**Evidence from Student Writing**		
Includes specific participants, such as people, animals, objects.	Names the garden plants (parsley, white Russian kale, etc.) and tools (cultivator, garden weasel, ruler). x		

Figure 6.5 (continued)

Criteria	Evidence of Criteria in Student Writing	Score		
		3	2	1
Uses simple past tense (e.g., *we walked, they sang, the ducks waddled*).	*Went, planted, used, watered* (appropriately mixes reporting of plants' growth using present tense: *are sprouting, are planted*), includes other language features in the same clause that do not retell or define ("cultivates means it looks like a claw").		x	
Uses mostly action verbs (e.g., doing, saying, showing verbs such as *painted, called, watered*).	*Planted, used, watered, sprouting, went, spread, looseing,* includes a mental/thinking verb: *know.*	x		
Includes linking items that show time, sequence, and location (e.g., *first, next, later, then, on, in*).	Uses *and* to link clauses.			x
Details are relevant to purpose.	All details explain the actions, includes unit vocabulary that provides image of garden and specific details to support the action.	x		
For personal recount, uses first-person pronouns (*I, we*).	Uses *I* to begin most clauses, as well as *we.*		x	

Criterion	Notes		
Includes clear linking between pronouns and referents (classmates = they) that provide cohesion.	Generally demonstrates understanding (e.g., Class = we, Lettce = they). There were many lettuce plants sprouting in the garden, but this is not clear in this text. Cultivator = it, cultivates = it (incorrect usage).	x	
Includes conventions of spelling and punctuation.	Spells unit/garden vocabulary correctly and controls many common as well as specific spellings, incorrect spellings include: *sped* for *spread*, *now* for *know*, *Lettce* for *lettuce*, *planing* for *planting* (once incorrectly once correctly), *looseing* for *loosening*. Pattern seems to be leaving out one letter. Could be rushing; check on this.\n\nNo use of periods and capital letters that divide clauses into sentences.	x	x

Connecting Language Features to Student Performance Using Rubrics

As mentioned earlier, rubrics are another useful tool for providing teachers with the data they need in order to offer explicit support and direction for struggling writers. However, even the most carefully constructed rubrics do not guarantee success. How rubrics are used sends a message to young writers. If the rubric becomes the purpose—instead of a tool—the point of writing is lost (Wray and Lewis 1997). Students tend to drop the meaning and personal investment attached to the act of writing when the point of writing becomes achieving the highest possible score. Rubrics used for instructional planning work best if students are involved in their design and interpretation. Many teachers construct writing rubrics with their students as instructional scaffolds. Sometimes, teachers also encourage students to use rubrics as part of a process of self-assessment as they present their writing drafts during peer or teacher conferences. If student-teacher dialogue is based on evidence and criteria, explicit discussion of the specific information needed to write in multiple genres becomes routine and constently exposes young writers to concrete knowledge about text. Figure 6.6 provides a "student friendly" rubric as an example of an instrument developed for this purpose.

Moving from Assessment to Instruction

The rubrics we have presented here are part of a process in which teachers explicitly link assessment and instruction. Helping students identify language features for commonly used patterns that fit specific functions is important if young writers are ultimately going to learn to control language for their own purposes. The assessment practices described in this section illustrate one way that teachers can

A Classroom Teacher's Guide to Struggling Writers

work with students to identify the criteria that best fit the classroom writing context. To begin, we suggest that teachers:

- Identify the expectations for writing in a specific area.
- Clarify the language features that students need to learn to control to be effective writers for particular purposes.
- Create rubrics that highlight these features.
- Utilize rubrics in dialogue with students to drive instruction and to demonstrate what students know and can do.

Explicitly teaching that many language patterns fit both personal and academic purposes is important for many children, especially struggling students or English language learners who have not internalized the structural forms of English as a primary language. In the list on pages 98–99, we have noted the language patterns that make a personal recount effective. Students need to see that they are always making choices that help their intended audience understand what they are trying to say both inside and outside of school. Email for example might contain "formal" letter like language, such as "Dear Ms. Moran" for a teacher, but might be more familiar "Hey Buddy" for a friend. If students examine these differences we are preparing them to understand distinctions between "everyday" colloquial language and more formal structures mostly found in "school language." Studies show that this differentiation is key to students development of the concepts and language they need for academic success (Schleppegrell and Go 2007; Gebhard, Harman, and Seger 2007). Contrasting language variations as part of the writing curriculum helps students consider that home dialects are distinct from academic language, but both are equally valuable for their purposes. At the same time, it is important to ensure that students realize that a genre-focused rubric is not a template to be filled but a guide with tools for the writer's use. In fact, in Kobe's writing, he effectively drew on features such as description and explanation (e.g., he described the garden tools used and elaborated on *why* the cultivator was needed) from other academic genres to *engage* and *inform* next year's students about the gardening activity.

Figure 6.6 "Student Friendly" Recount Rubric

Purpose: Recount, writing that tells *what happened*

Audience: Why am I writing this recount? What is it about? Who will read it?

Criteria **How will I make my recount effective for my audience?**	**Description**	**Score 3 – My text meets all criteria.** **Score 2 – My text meets some criteria.** **Score 1 – My text does not include criteria. Explain your score.**
Orientation:	My opening helps my reader *imagine* the time, place, and location of the event by telling who, when, where.	
Series of Events:	My piece lists a series of events in order with language that elaborates on each event. I included quotes or dialogue to help show my point of view or that of my participants.	
Conclusion or Reflection:	I don't just list the events that happened; I also share my own ideas or opinions during my recount and in the conclusion.	

Language Features:	
I name specific participants, such as people, animals, and objects.	
I use the past tense (e.g., *we walked, they sang, the ducks waddled*).	
I use a lot of action verbs.	
I use connector words to show when and where events happened and in what order (e.g., *first, next, later, then, on, in*).	
I include details that illustrate my key events.	
I use *I* and *we* to show that this tells about a personal experience.	
I've checked my spelling.	
I use periods, question marks, exclamation points, and quotation marks.	

Summary

In this chapter, we have shared how teachers can work in groups to explore dimensions of the student as composer, editor, and author. We also demonstrated how rubrics can be created to clarify for teachers and students the criteria for effective writing. Finally, we have suggested the benefits of using ongoing assessment directly with students in the form of focused feedback shared in conferences and in other interactions between teachers and students, such as minilessons and small-group discussions. (See Chapter 4 for more on conferences.) The list below suggests additional assessment resources that teachers may use to build on these ideas.

Additional Assessment Resources

Akhavan, N. 2004. *How to Align Literacy Instruction, Assessment, and Standards and Achieve Results You Never Dreamed Possible.* Portsmouth, NH: Heinemann.

Hurley, S. R., and J. V. Tinajero. 2001. *Literacy Assessment of Second Language Learners.* New York: Allyn and Bacon.

O'Malley, J. M., and L. V. Pierce. 1996. *Authentic Assessment for English Language Learners, Practical Approaches for Teachers.* New York: Addison-Wesley.

Rhodes, L. 1992. *Literacy Assessment: A Handbook of Instruments.* Portsmouth, NH: Heinemann.

Stefanakis, E. H. 2001. *Multiple Intelligences and Portfolios: A Window into the Learner's Mind.* Portsmouth, NH: Heinemann.

Taberski, S. 2000. *On Solid Ground: Strategies for Teaching Reading K–3.* Portsmouth, NH: Heinemann.

Spelling and Other Writing "Skills"

Perhaps the most noticeable characteristic of struggling writers is that they are often poor spellers (Graham, Harris, and Larsen 2001; Silliman, Jimerson, and Wilkinson 2000; Tompkins 2002). For this reason, writing instruction for struggling writers tends to focus heavily on spelling and other writing mechanics. However, an overemphasis on writing mechanics, including spelling, will undermine the writing development of struggling writers by limiting their opportunities to engage in meaningful writing (Englert and Raphael 1988; Graham, Harris, and Larsen 2001). An overemphasis on spelling may also lead to "dull, vapid writing devoid of the writer's voice [that], no matter how well spelled and punctuated, will have little communicative effect beyond demonstrating the writer's mastery of the conventions" (Murphy and Dudley-Marling 2000, 201).

However, none of this diminishes the importance of learning to spell. Spelling is valued above all other writing conventions in our culture (Beckham-Hungler and Williams 2003). It affects the appearance of writing (Glazer 1994) and, significantly, "poor spellers jeopardize the rhetorical effect of their writing" (Murphy and Dudley-Marling 2000, 201). Put simply, poorly spelled pieces are less effective.

Spelling proficiency also affects writing fluency. That is, good spellers tend to write more (Graham and Harris 1997), and writers who are overly focused on spelling will have a difficult time keeping track of their intentions. Therefore, explicit attention to spelling instruction is a high priority for teachers of struggling writers. Yet it is important to recognize that this instruction is most effective when it is embedded in a routine writing program in which students are pushed to write for a wide range of audiences and purposes. In this context, students learn to spell conventionally because it contributes to the effectiveness of their writing for different purposes and audiences.

Given the prominence of spelling—and writing mechanics more generally—for struggling writers, we've dedicated an entire chapter to discuss these issues. Our focus will be on instructional strategies, but we begin by sharing some characteristics of good spellers and poor spellers that have clear instructional implications.

Characteristics of Good Spellers and Poor Spellers

In a longitudinal study that followed a group of students from kindergarten through sixth grade, Margaret Hughes and Dennis Searle (1997) identified a number of important differences between good spellers and poor spellers. In general, good spellers knew how to spell more words conventionally than poor spellers, although, on average, poor spellers managed to spell 65 percent of the words in their writing correctly. Good spellers also distinguished themselves by the approach they took to spelling unfamiliar words. We'll say more about this in the section that follows.

Among the characteristics that differentiated good spellers from poor spellers, Hughes and Searle identified the following:

> ***Good spellers are more likely than poor spellers to be avid readers.*** Readers often learn how words are spelled in the process of reading (Smith 1982). Reading more frequently (and usually more

proficiently) gives avid readers a distinct advantage in spelling. Still, although good spellers who are poor readers may be rare, there are poor spellers who are good, avid readers. This latter finding suggests that poor spellers tend to read differently than good spellers.

Good spellers read like writers. Frank Smith (1981, 1982) stressed the importance of reading in writing development, arguing that reading is the primary source of knowledge about writing. Good spellers not only read more than poor spellers, they are also more likely to note various conventions (spelling, punctuation) in the process of reading.

Good spellers have a sense of spelling as a system. According to Hughes and Searle, poor spellers tend to see English spellings as arbitrary. It's easy to see how they might reach this conclusion. English words often include letters that don't represent any sound (e.g., *bomb, lamb, sign, gnu, cave, rain*); some sounds are represented by different letters or letter combinations (e.g., *some/us, fall/phone, staff/laugh*); many letters, particularly vowels, represent more than one sound (e.g., *sign/sing, son/song/so, along/ate/at/all*); and, reliable spelling "rules" often don't work (*chief*, for example, contradicts the rule "when two vowels go walking, the first does the talking"). Hughes and Searle also note that children who view English spellings as unreliable and chaotic—as poor spellers appear to do—are more likely to rely on memorization to learn spellings.

Yet, contrary to appearances, English spellings are fairly predictable if meaning *and* letter-sound relationships are taken into account. English spellings may not be perfectly regular, but there is a good deal of predictability in the system. Words that mean the same thing, for example, tend to be spelled in the same way (e.g., *sign/signal, bomb/bombastic*) (Templeton 2003). Similarly, there may be several possible letters or letter combinations for representing different English sounds, but the alternatives are limited. For example, there are several choices for representing /f/ (as in *fun*), but in the end, there are only four possibilities (*f, ff, ph, gh*), even fewer when the position of the sound within the word is taken into account (e.g., only *f* and *ph* represent /f/ in the initial position). Spelling by analogy (e.g., *light, bright, right*) is generally an effective strategy for spelling unknown words and, where there are exceptions (e.g., *kite, bite*), again, the choices are limited. Good spellers, who recognize that the English spelling system is generally predictable, have an easier time learning to spell new words than poor spellers, who may attempt to memorize every new word.

Good spellers are self-reliant. Hughes and Searle found that good spellers, compared to poor spellers, were more likely to rely on their own resources when attempting to spell words they didn't know. Specifically, good spellers were more likely to use their knowledge of the regularities of the English spelling system to "have a go" (Turbill 2000) at unfamiliar spellings (e.g., *egreejous* for *egregious*). Poor spellers, on the other hand, tended to pester teachers or classmates to spell words for them.

Good spellers generate multiple spellings. Hughes and Searle also found that a common strategy among good spellers attempting to spell unfamiliar words was to generate multiple spellings and pick the one that "looked right." A good speller attempting to spell "egregious," for example, might generate several versions (e.g., "agregous," "egregous," and "egregious") and pick the one that *looked* right ("egregious"). In contrast, poor spellers rarely use this strategy.

Hughes and Searle's conception of good spellers goes beyond traditional notions that good spellers distinguish themselves merely by spelling more words correctly than poorer spellers, presumably because they have better memories or better phonics skills. Rather, Hughes and Searle found that good spellers augment memorization with problem-solving strategies that draw on their knowledge of the predictable aspects of English spellings. Still, they found that these problem-solving strategies are not fully developed even among good spellers until around sixth grade. Overall, Hughes and Searle document a process of learning to spell that goes well beyond the accumulation of words that have been memorized or sounds that have been mastered. Good spellers use a range of skills and strategies in the process of spelling and learning to spell.

Traditional Approaches

This section briefly examines two traditional approaches to spelling instruction: spelling lists and teacher corrections. Although popular, these approaches actually have little theoretical or research support and, therefore, ought to be used sparingly, if at all.

Spelling Lists

Although there was a move away from commercial spelling programs in the 1980s and 1990s, basal spellers remain the focus of spelling instruction in the majority of classrooms in the United States (Fresch 2003). Serious questions have been raised about the effectiveness of basal spelling programs, however (Beckham-Hungler and Williams 2003; Wilde 1991). Many students perform well on weekly spelling tests, for example, but still misspell many of the same words in their spontaneous writing. Worse, spelling lists and weekly spelling tests emphasize memorization, a particular problem for poor spellers, who overrely on memorizing spelling words. Some teachers have introduced individualized, personal spellings lists as an alternative to basal spellers, but even personal spelling lists have limited potential (Beckham-Hungler and Williams 2003).

Memorization does have a place in spelling instruction for struggling writers, but only if it is augmented by activities that encourage a problem-solving stance (Snowball and Bolton 1999). As Templeton (2003) puts it, "Spelling is not a rote memory task but instead a process of abstracting patterns" (746). Therefore, the best instruction focuses on helping students uncover those patterns.

Teacher Corrections

Most of us recall teachers who routinely corrected all of our misspellings. Since most of us are good spellers, it is tempting to conclude that teachers' corrections were instrumental in our spelling development. Certainly, it is helpful for teachers to function as editors, making final corrections to student writing before it is shared with a wider audience. Explicit feedback on the spelling of a small number of particularly troublesome words is also helpful, especially if that feedback is followed up in individual spelling lessons. However, in general, extensive correction of students' mechanical errors, including spelling, is supported by neither theory nor research (Farnan and Dahl 2003). In fact, heavy correction of students' spelling encourages their dependence on their teachers (Glasswell, Parr, and McNaughton 2003), a particular problem for struggling writers. Further, teachers who mark up students' writing with corrections (spelling, punctuation, and so forth) may prompt students to limit their writing to words they already know how to spell or, in the worst case, discourage students from writing at all. We recommend that teachers resist the red pen and, instead, use students' misspellings as assessment data to inform future instructional support. For example, if a student regularly fails to use a silent *e* or vowel digraphs (e.g., *flee*, *heave*) to mark vowels as long (e.g., *hat* for *hate*, *slid* for *slide*, *fle* for *flea*), the teacher might plan a series of lessons with the student to focus on this issue. If this is a problem for a number of students in the class, the teacher could consider whole-class minilessons and/or small-group lessons to focus on orthographic conventions for marking vowels as long.

In general, there has been much confusion about the issue of "correctness" in the context of writing workshop. Correctness matters and students must learn to edit and revise their writing. Misspelled words and other mechanical errors undermine the effectiveness of any piece of writing. The evidence indicates, however, that overzealous correction of students' writing is not an effective strategy for teaching spelling, particularly for struggling writers. The aim is not about emphasizing correctness, but employing the best strategies for helping students become effective writers, which demands proofreading and spelling skills.

Instructional Strategies

We now turn our attention to effective instructional strategies for which there is theoretical and research support.

A Classroom Teacher's Guide to Struggling Writers

Word Study

Word study activities focus students' attention on sounds, syllables, morphemes, and words. The emphasis, however, is always on searching for generalizable patterns, particularly how spelling patterns relate to word meanings. As mentioned, a problem-solving approach to spelling instruction is particularly important for struggling writers, who tend to overrely on memorization for learning to spell new words. Poetry, rhyming games, alphabet books, and so on focus on regularities of the English sound system. (See Bear, Invernizzi, Templeton, and Johnston 2008 for a comprehensive discussion of activities for word study.)

Other activities for word study focus on word derivations, including prefixes and suffixes. A fifth-grade teacher we know uses semantic mapping to study word derivations. The example in Figure 7.1 illustrates a semantic map of words derived from *graph*.

Similar lessons can be constructed at any grade level. We've seen first graders, for example, brainstorm words derived from *catch* (*catching, catcher, catches*), *play* (*plays, playing, playful, playmate, played*), and *jump* (*jumped, jumps, jumper, jumping*), for example.

Word Sorts

Words sorts are a particularly useful example of word play that can be used to help children learn to spell by analogy (Hodges 2003). In this case, students study words looking for similarities and differences, formulating "tentative hypotheses about spelling patterns as they group words into categories" (Fresch 2000, 346). Typically, teachers provide sets of words printed on cards. These sets emphasize different word features or patterns. Teachers may ask students to sort words according to specified criteria, or they may ask students to generate their own categories. Some of the word features we've seen teachers highlight in word sorts include:

- Onsets (initial sounds) and rimes (word families) (e.g., -*ight*/-*ite*, -*art*/-*ale*).
- Final sounds (e.g., *quake*/*duck*, *nice*/*hops*, *print*/*cent*).
- Short/long vowels (e.g., *mad*/*made*, *grip*/*gripe*).
- Consonant digraphs (e.g., *ph, sh, ch, th*).

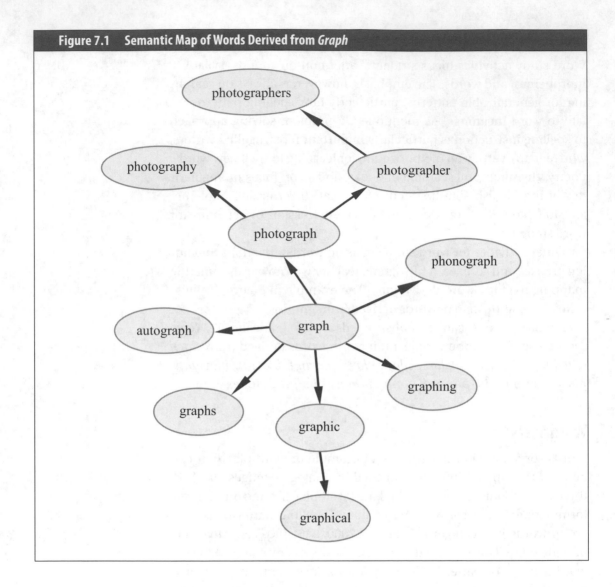

Figure 7.1   Semantic Map of Words Derived from _Graph_

- Vowel digraphs (e.g., _b<u>ea</u>d_, _d<u>ea</u>d_, _b<u>oa</u>t_, _f<u>ee</u>t_, _b<u>ay</u>_, _tr<u>ai</u>t_, _b<u>oil</u>_).
- Prefixes and suffixes (e.g., _pre-_, _re-_, _-ness_, _-er_).
- Singular and plural (e.g., _dog/dogs, cat/cats, glass/glasses, child/ children_).

In an example cited by Fresch (2000), students in a fifth-grade inclusion class were asked to sort words illustrating various ways of representing the long *i* sound: *night, bright, flight, right, twice, wise, nine, smile, prize, fly, try* (346). Students could also be asked to sort words according to meanings, emphasizing the principle that words that have similar meanings tend to be spelled the same way (e.g., *sign, signal, signature; bomb, bombard, bombastic, bombardier*).

Spelling Minilessons

Teachers can introduce any of these effective strategies during whole-class minilessons. In fact, some spelling lessons are particularly well suited to a whole-class format. When Curt Dudley-Marling taught third grade, for example, he scheduled five- to ten-minute whole-class spelling lessons each morning before recess. Usually these were based on various forms of word play, including sorting activities. For example, when he observed that several students in his class overgeneralized the use of *ff* to represent the /*f*/ sound in the final position (e.g., *laff, graff, leaff*), he did a series of minilessons on the /*f*/ sound. He first challenged his students to come up with all the words they could think of that ended with /*f*/. As they suggested words, he asked his students to spell them. When Melissa suggested "leaf" she offered the following spelling: "l-e-f-f." Mr. Dudley-Marling commented, "Yes, it sounds like it could be spelled with an *f-f*, but it is actually spelled with a single *f*." Then he wrote *l-e-a-f* on chart paper. He also noted for the class that, in this case, the long *e* sound is represented by *e-a*, which they would talk about in a different minilesson. As students continued to suggest words that end with /*f*/, they created a list and classified them as shown in Figure 7.2.

Dudley-Marling followed up this lesson the next day by asking his students if they could determine a "rule" that could account for the different ways of representing the /*f*/ sound at the end of words. Although this proved difficult, a couple of students suggested that single-syllable words with a short vowel sound seemed to be spelled –*ff*, although another student noted two exceptions (*graph, deaf*). A third student made this observation: "Words that ended with two letters, like *wolf* and *barf*, used just one *f*." Dudley-Marling concluded the lesson by commenting that, for many words ending with the /*f*/ sound, writers have to remember which letter or letter combinations are used to represent the sound. He also taped the chart paper on

Figure 7.2   Spelling Minilesson

-ff	*-ph*	*-gh*	*-f*
off	photograph	laugh	deaf
puff	telegraph	rough	leaf
huff	graph	tough	reef
stuff			beef
sniff			wolf
handcuff			barf
			chief
			chef

the blackboard and invited students to add words ending with the /f/ sound as they encountered them in their reading.

Have-a-Go Spellings

Whole-class spelling minilessons are also a good place for teachers to model strategies used by good spellers (Turbill 2000). We've observed teachers "stretching out" the sounds of words to illustrate *have-a-go* spellings, which have also been called *invented spellings*. For example, the teacher might say, "Listen to the sounds in *broken*: buh[B]—rrr[R]—oh[O]—kuh[K]—eh[E]—nnn[N]." Teachers might also model breaking words into syllables to facilitate have-a-go spellings, since many poor spellers fail to use this simple strategy.

A Classroom Teacher's Guide to Struggling Writers

It is important that poor spellers learn to rely on their own resources for spelling unknown words, and that all school-age children, even the poorest spellers, have at least some knowledge of English orthography on which to draw. Even if students are able to represent only a few sounds independently in words they're trying to spell (e.g., *DG* for *dog*), this is preferable to relying on others for accurate spellings. Still, teachers may have to work individually with students to help them have a go at spelling unknown words, following up with the kind of strategies outlined in the minilessons we discussed earlier. When students learn to work with the sound system of English spellings in this way, they also advance their development of phonics skills (Adams 1990; Richgels 2001).

Proofreading

There is a strong relationship between spelling and proofreading skills. Students with good proofreading skills learn to spell new words by reading like writers who notice spelling and other conventions as they read. Teaching proofreading also addresses the problem that many poor spellers misspell words in their writing that they spell correctly on spelling lists (Beckham-Hungler and Williams 2003). Jan Turbill (2000) found that proofreading is an effective way to address the curious finding that many poor spellers—even adults—spell many "hard" words correctly while consistently misspelling relatively easier words. She concluded that poor spellers often get the hard words right because they give these words more of their attention. Teaching students to proofread their work, she found, proved to be an effective way to improve students' spelling in the context of their writing. In Turbill's words, proofreading helps even young elementary students develop a "spelling conscience."

Proofreading must be explicitly taught, however. Here are some strategies for teaching proofreading to students:

- Copy a piece of writing onto an overhead transparency and then model proofreading strategies during whole-class minilessons.

- Model multiple readings of a single piece of writing as a proofreading strategy. The evidence indicates that reading a text more than once is a more effective proofreading strategy than, say, reading texts backward (Hodges 2003).

- With permission from the student, copy a piece of a student's unedited writing onto an overhead transparency along with paper copies for the whole class. Alternatively, teachers could produce a piece of their own writing with some words deliberately misspelled. Model proofreading the first few lines of the writing and then ask students to continue the process in pairs. After students have finished, return to the whole group to compare notes.

- Ask students to keep a list of words they frequently misspell and encourage them to find these words in their reading, looking closely to see how they are spelled (Turbill 2000).

- Provide lots of opportunities for students to write for a range of real audiences. Most people, including children, give greater attention to spelling when writing for real audiences.

Frank Smith (1982) argues that there is a tension between composition (the creative production of text) and transcription (getting the word down "on paper"). To some degree, this supports the idea of teaching spelling as a proofreading skill. In early drafts, getting the words down on paper, even if spelled incorrectly, is critical to composing effective writing. The flow of ideas must not be hostage to writing conventions. Still, it does novice writers little good to "get the words down" if they can't be read later. So learning to spell well—without having to direct attention away from the flow of ideas—is a critical factor in becoming a fluent writer.

Spelling Journals

Jan Turbill (2000) recommends that students use spelling journals for have-a-go spellings. With this approach, teachers encourage students to record words causing them trouble; look for these words in their reading; and then, when they encounter them, write down the conventional spelling in their notebooks. Other teachers we know ask students to keep personalized spelling dictionaries, listing commonly used words they regularly misspell. Spelling journals are also places where students can record interesting or unusual spellings, perhaps for later whole-class discussion. As an alternative to spelling journals, some teachers have students create personal spelling dictionaries on index cards.

A Classroom Teacher's Guide to Struggling Writers

Reading and More Reading

Reading provides developing spellers with a rich source of data on conventional English spellings. Even adults often learn how words are spelled by seeing them in print. Poor readers will, however, always be at an extreme disadvantage learning to spell. Many students, especially poor spellers, need the explicit support of their teachers to learn how to *read like a writer*, as Frank Smith (1982) has put it. Students who read like writers attend to the conventions of good writing that they will use in their own writing. Students will benefit, for example, from teachers modeling how good spellers "notice" spellings as they read. Elementary teachers might conduct a series of minilessons in which they read aloud passages they have projected on an overhead, perhaps providing students with photocopies of the passages they'll be reading. As teachers read, they might pause occasionally to talk about what they notice about interesting spellings. For instance, pausing over the word *penguin*, a teacher might say, "Isn't that interesting. *Penguin* is spelled *p-e-n-g-u-i-n*, and not *p-e-n-g-w-i-n*, which is how it sounds." Importantly, teachers should follow up these minilessons with small-group and individual lessons for poor spellers.

Other Strategies for Teaching Spelling

The following list provides additional suggestions for teaching spelling to students.

- Ask students to circle words in their writing if they're unsure of the spellings. This encourages students to develop a visual sense of words and promotes proofreading skills. Teachers can also use the circled words for follow-up lessons or, perhaps, ask students to look up the correct spellings for some or all of these words.

- Encourage students to generate several alternative spellings for unknown words and then select the spelling that looks best. Again, this helps students develop a visual sense of words and encourages the development of phonetic skills.

- Use word walls that include commonly misspelled words.

- Encourage students to look for misspellings in the writing that appears around the classroom (e.g., chart stories, written directions).

- Have students examine and discuss how advertisers deliberately misspell words to attract attention (e.g., *lite, kampground, brite, snaks, cheez, kat, pleez*) (Turbill 2000).

- Ask older students to identify unconventional spellings commonly used in informal, out-of-school writing genres such as Instant Messaging and email for in-class discussion.

- Play games such as hangman, Spill 'n Spell, Scrabble, crossword puzzles, word scrambles, anagrams, and so on that focus students' attention on spelling.

- Give students a long word and challenge them to spell as many words as possible using its letters (e.g., *prediction: red, tin, pin, predict, diction, no, not*).

- Use word hunts to challenge students to find instances of particular words around the classroom.

Fluent Writing: Handwriting, Keyboarding, and Spell Checkers

Students who are overly focused on forming letters or words will have difficulty directing their attention to the composing process. Therefore, the development of fluent handwriting is also an important factor in fluent writing. As Don Graves (1983) put it, "When handwriting flows, the writer has better access to his own thoughts and information" (181). Illegible handwriting can undermine the communicative effectiveness of any piece of writing. Therefore, an effective writing program provides students with explicit instruction in handwriting. Even in a world with ready access to computer word processing, it seems likely that handwriting will remain an important skill. There are many programs available for teaching handwriting.

Additionally, for many students, especially students with chronic sensorimotor problems, using a word-processing program to compose can positively affect their writing fluency. Ultimately, all students may be better off learning to compose with word processors since keyboarding is, potentially, much faster than handwriting. However,

A Classroom Teacher's Guide to Struggling Writers

to realize the potential of word processors on writing fluency, children need explicit instruction in keyboarding skills (Farnan and Dahl 2003). The "hunt-and-peck" typing method offers few advantages over handwriting. There are many fun and effective software programs available commercially for teaching keyboarding to young children.

On the face of it, word processors offer another advantage to young writers and poor spellers: spell checkers. Spell checkers instantly identify—and, in some cases, automatically correct—spelling errors. However, spell checkers are primarily an editing tool that is most useful to competent spellers. Writers still need to correct the spelling errors that are identified by spell checkers, and they still need to recognize misspellings that the spell checkers miss, such as substituting *then* for *than*. For this reason, spell checkers at best augment but cannot replace the need for frequent, intensive, individualized, and explicit spelling instruction.

Punctuation and Capitalization

Punctuation carries a good dealing of meaning in writing. Writers use various conventions—commas, periods, exclamation marks, capitalization, paragraphing, and so on—to organize ideas and signal meanings not present in words themselves, all for the benefit of readers. Writers who cannot use punctuation appropriately risk confusing or misleading their readers, which undermines the communicative effectiveness of their writing. Yet, many adults have difficulty with the use of commas, colons, and semicolons. Not surprisingly, problems with punctuation are characteristic of many poor writers (Graham, Harris, and Larsen 2001).

Learning to punctuate, like learning to spell, is, to some degree, developmental. Sandra Wilde (1991) observed that "children's hypotheses about punctuation grow out of their experience and evolve over time" (119). In our experience, young children's use of periods, for example, can range from periods placed almost randomly, placed after each word, placed at the end of each line, placed at the end of each page, and placed at the end of each phrase. All of these hypotheses make some sense. It is easy to see how young students using basal readers, for example, might conclude that periods come at the end of every line or even every word, and, to very young readers, the placement of periods might indeed seem random (Rhodes and Dudley-Marling 1996).

The principal source of data informing children's emergent use of punctuation will come from their reading. This observation suggests an important point. Children will learn to punctuate effectively in the context of a rich program of reading with the support of teachers who help students *notice* punctuation and generate hypotheses about how various forms of punctuation work to affect meaning.

It is equally important that punctuation be taught in the context of authentic student writing, where the appropriate use of punctuation affects writers' intentions. It makes sense, for example, to teach the use of quotation marks when students begin to use dialogue in their writing; that is, the ideal time to teach quotation marks is when students *need* quotation marks in their writing. Calkins and Graves (1980) found that teaching punctuation outside the context of students' writing—as a set of definitions and rules, for example—is much less effective than teaching punctuation to help students fulfill their intentions (to persuade, to entertain, to report, etc.). There are at least two reasons for this finding. The first is that the "simple" punctuation rules most of us were taught in school really aren't so simple. A period may go at the end of every sentence, but *sentence* defies easy definition. Many of us were taught that a sentence is a complete thought, usually containing a noun phrase and a verb phrase. Yet a sentence can range from a single word, such as *Stop*, to incredibly complex sentences containing multiple subjects and clauses. And some writers deliberately violate these rules for effect. From a linguistic point of view, *sentence* is a very complex notion. The advice to place periods at places in the text where "you hear your voice drop" is equally problematic, since some dialects mark the end of at least some sentences with rising intonation.

Second, even though it will be difficult for children to learn a precise, explicit definition of *sentence* or simple rules for the placement of periods, the relationship between *learning about* and *learning how* is uneven. Learning definitions about punctuation or grammar—*learning about*—is not the same as learning to use language forms in the context of actual writing—*learning how*. Still, explicit instruction in the use of periods and other punctuation is necessary and useful if it's connected to students' actual writing and intentions.

A Classroom Teacher's Guide to Struggling Writers

In the rest of this section, we offer some examples of contextualized punctuation instruction. Interested readers might also consult Sandra Wilde's book *You Kan Red This! Spelling and Punctuation for Whole Language Classrooms, K–6* (1991) as well as Janet Angelillo's *A Fresh Approach to Teaching Punctuation* (2002) for more detailed discussions of teaching punctuation.

Examples of Contextualized Punctuation Instruction

It's probably never too early to draw children's attention to punctuation marks and how they work. Lisa Cleaveland, for example, emphasizes the punctuation her first-grade students encounter in their reading (Ray and Cleaveland 2005). For instance, Ms. Cleaveland teaches dashes and ellipses to her first graders because her students frequently encounter these forms in the picture books they read.

In the context of a writing minilesson, Ms. Cleaveland asked her students to consider why an author had used dashes to write *slowly* as *s-l-o-w-l-y*. Her students had no trouble guessing that the author used dashes to get her readers to read the word *slowly* slowly.

In another minilesson, Ms. Cleaveland talked with students about using ellipses in their writing. During sharing time she sometimes asked her students to talk about how they used punctuation in their writing and why. Ms. Cleaveland also posted a chart in her classroom listing the different kinds of punctuation students had used. During all discussions of punctuation, Ms. Cleaveland stressed the ultimate goal of considering the readers' needs. In other words, she always encouraged students to use punctuation directly in response to how they wanted readers to read their texts.

In addition to dashes and ellipses, young students are also likely to encounter periods, question marks, exclamation marks, apostrophes, commas, and quotation marks in their reading. In a very real sense, teachers and authors coteach the use of writing conventions. For example, to help students examine the use of question marks, teachers could share *Brown Bear, Brown Bear, What Do You See?* (Martin and Carle 1996) during whole-class minilessons, guided reading groups, or individual reading conferences. *The Day Jimmy's Boa Ate the Wash* (Noble and Kellogg 1992) is one of many good books for illustrating the use of quotation marks. Virtually, every children's book offers guidance in the use of periods and capitalization. Big Books are a particularly good resource for illustrating the use of various forms of punctuation in whole-class lessons. In general, children's literature is an excellent source of data about the range of punctuation students are likely to use in their own writing.

Students' writing also provides good material to introduce or support a discussion about punctuation and to reinforce previous whole-class or individual lessons. Teachers or students can read students' writing out loud to illustrate how punctuation gives readers cues. For example, perhaps a student's writing does not include punctuation. If the teacher or student reads the text aloud without pausing or making changes in intonation, the student will likely suggest places to add periods, commas, and, possibly, question marks.

Many teachers we visit sometimes copy their own or students' writing (with their permission, of course) onto overhead transparencies for whole-class minilessons on punctuation. Using their own writing, teachers might talk about how they selected punctuation to serve the needs of readers. Alternatively, teachers might present a sample of their writing without punctuation as a means of initiating a conversation about where to place punctuation (and why). Similarly, the class can review a sample of student writing to discuss how punctuation was used (and not used) to communicate the writer's intentions.

We've also seen teachers challenge their students to examine the use of punctuation through "punctuation hunts." One second-grade teacher told her students she would give them fifteen minutes to find and document uses of commas in the classroom. When she asked how they might proceed, several suggested looking at books as well as print posted around the classroom. After the students returned to the whole group, they shared their examples, discussed how commas were used, and then speculated on the general purpose of commas.

Finally, Sandra Wilde (1991) notes that teachers may want to refresh their own knowledge of punctuation. Many dictionaries offer useful explanations, along with illustrative examples, of the uses of punctuation marks.

Summary

Encouraging students to write for different purposes increases their need to learn and use punctuation and correct spelling. Ultimately, the goal of instruction is to help students develop an intuitive understanding of how correct spelling and the use of punctuation work to support their intentions as writers and to support the needs of their readers. As noted, learning definitions of punctuation—such as periods or commas—has an uncertain relationship to using these punctuation forms in the context of authentic writing. Students are most likely to develop this intuitive understanding in the context of their own writing in a writing program that stresses effective writing: writing that fulfills the writer's communicative intentions. In the end, "dull, vapid writing devoid of the writer's voice, not matter how well spelled and punctuated, will have little communicative effect beyond demonstrating the writer's mastery of the conventions" (Murphy and Dudley-Marling 2000, 201).

References

Adams, M. J. 1990. *Beginning to Read: Thinking and Learning About Print.* Cumberland, RI: MIT Press.

Akhavan, N. 2004. *How to Align Literacy Instruction, Assessment, and Standards and Achieve Results You Never Dreamed Possible.* Portsmouth, NH: Heinemann.

Angelillo, J. 2002. *A Fresh Approach to Teaching Punctuation.* New York: Scholastic.

Annandale, K., R. Bindon, J. Broz, J. Dougan, K. Handley, A. Johnston, L. Lockett, P. Lynch, and R. Rourke. 2006. *First Steps Second Edition: Writing Resource Book.* Beverly, MA: STEPS Professional Development.

Atwell, N. 1998. *In the Middle: New Understanding About Writing, Reading, and Learning.* Portsmouth, NH: Boynton/Cook.

Bear, D. R., M. Invernizzi, S. Templeton, and F. Johnston. 2008. *Words Their Way: Word Study for Phonics, Vocabulary, and Spelling Instruction.* 4th ed. Upper Saddle River, NJ: Pearson/ Prentice Hall.

Bearne, E. 2002. *Making Progress in Writing.* London: Routledge.

Beck, I. L., M. G. McKeown, R. L. Hamilton, and L. Kucan. 1997. *Questioning the Author: An Approach for Enhancing Student*

Engagement with Text. Newark, DE: International Reading Association.

Beckham-Hungler, D., and C. Williams. 2003. "Teaching Words that Students Misspell: Spelling Instruction and Young Children's Writing." *Language Arts* 80: 299–308.

Brannon, L., and C. H. Knoblauch. 1984. "On Students' Rights to Their Own Texts: A Model of Teacher Response." *College Composition and Communication* 33 (2): 157–66.

Britton, J., T. Burgess, N. Martin, A. McLeod, and H. Rosen. 1975. *The Development of Writing Abilities.* London: MacMillan.

Button, K., M. J. Johnson, and P. Furgerson. 1996. "Interactive Writing in a Primary Classroom." *The Reading Teacher* 49: 446–54.

Calkins, L. K. 1994. *The Art of Teaching Writing.* Portsmouth, NH: Heinemann.

Calkins, L., and D. H. Graves. 1980. "Research Update: When Children Want to Punctuate: Basic Skills Belong in Context." *Language Arts* 57: 567–73.

Carini, P., and M. Himley. 2000. *From Another Angle: Children's Strengths and School Standards.* New York: Teachers College Press.

Chapman, M. L. 1999. "Situated, Social, Active: Rewriting Genre in the Elementary Classroom." *Written Communication* 16: 469–90.

Choi, Y. 2003. *The Name Jar.* Edmund, OK: Dragonfly Publishing.

Cochran-Smith, M., and S. Lytle. 1999. "Relationships of Knowledge and Practice: Teacher Learning in Communities." In *Review of Research in Education, Volume 24,* edited by Iran-Nejad and C. D. Pearson, 251–307. Washington, DC: American Educational Research Association.

Cohen, E. G. 1994. *Designing Groupwork: Strategies for the Heterogeneous Classroom.* New York: Teachers College Press.

Cornerstone Initiative. 2008. *Knowledgeable Other Series: January 2008.* Retrieved December 9, 2008 from www.cornerstoneliteracy.org/video.html.

Cronin, D., and B. Lewin. 2000. *Click, Clack, Moo: Cows that Type.* New York: Simon and Schuster.

Derewianka, B. 1990. *Exploring How Texts Work.* Australia: Primary English Teaching Association.

Donovan, C. A., and L. B. Smolkin. 2002. "Children's Genre Knowledge: An Examination of K–5 Students' Performance on Multiple Tasks Providing Differing Levels of Scaffolding." *Reading Research Quarterly* 37 (4): 428–65.

Dudley-Marling, C. 1997. *Living with Uncertainty: The Messy Reality of Classroom Practice.* Portsmouth, NH: Heinemann.

Dudley-Marling, C., and J. Oppenheimer. 1995. "Writing and Ownership: A Critical Tale." *International Journal of Qualitative Studies in Education* 8: 281–95.

Dudley-Marling, C., and P. Paugh. 2005. "The Rich Get Richer, the Poor Get Direct Instruction." In *Reading for Profit,* edited by B. Altwerger, 156–71. Portsmouth, NH: Heinemann.

———. 2004. *A Classroom Teacher's Guide to Teaching Struggling Readers.* Portsmouth, NH: Heinemann.

Dufresne, M. 2007. *Snakes.* Amherst, MA: Pioneer Valley Press.

Dyson, A. H. 2001. "Writing and Children's Symbolic Repertoires: Development Unhinged." In *Handbook of Early Literacy Research,* edited by S. B. Neuman and D. K. Dickinson, 126–41. New York: Guilford.

———. 1993. *Social Worlds of Children Learning to Write in an Urban Primary School.* New York: Teachers College Press.

———. 1989. *Multiple Worlds of Child Writers: Friends Learning to Write.* New York: Teachers College Press.

Dyson, A. H., and S. W. Freedman. 2003. "Writing." In *Handbook of Research on the Teaching of English Language Arts,* edited by J. Flood, D. Lapp, J. R. Squire, and J. Jensen, 967–92. Mahwah, NJ: Erlbaum.

Emig, J. 1971. *The Composing Processes of Twelfth Graders.* Urbana, IL: National Council of Teachers of English.

Englert, C. S., and T. E. Raphael. 1988. "Constructing Well-Formed Prose: Process, Structure, and Metacognitive Knowledge." *Exceptional Children* 54: 513–20.

Farnan, N., and K. Dahl. 2003. "Children's Writing: Research and Practice." In *Handbook of Research on the Teaching of English*

Language Arts, edited by J. Flood, D. Lapp, J. R. Squire, and J. Jensen, 993–1007. Mahwah, NJ: Erlbaum.

Feelings, T. 1995. *The Middle Passage: White Ships/ Black Cargo.* New York: Dial.

Fink, L. S. n.d. *Once upon a Time Rethought: Writing Fractured Fairy Tales.* Retrieved May 28, 2008 from www.readwritethink.org /lessons/lesson_view.asp?id=853.

Fleishman, P. 2004. *Joyful Noise: Poems for Two Voices.* New York: HarperTrophy.

Fletcher, R., and Portalupi, J. 2001. *Writing Workshop: The Essential Guide.* Portsmouth, NH: Heinemann.

Fresch, M. J. 2003. "A National Survey of Spelling Instruction: Investigating Teachers' Beliefs and Practice." *Journal of Literary Research* Fall: accessed online May 25, 2006 from www.findarticles .com/p/articles/mi_qa3785/is_200310/ai_n9335174.

———. 2000. "What We Learned from Josh: Sorting Out Word Sorting." *Language Arts* 77: 232–40.

Gebhard, M., R. Harman, and W. Seger. 2007. "Reclaiming Recess: Learning the Language of Persuasion." *Language Arts* 84 (5): 419–30.

Gee, J. P. 1996. *Social Linguistics and Literacies: Ideology in Discourses.* 2d ed. New York: Taylor & Francis.

Gibbons, G. 1993. *From Seed to Plant.* New York: Holiday House.

Gibbons, P. 2002. *Scaffolding Language, Scaffolding Learning: Teaching Second Language Learners in the Mainstream Classroom.* Portsmouth, NH: Heinemann.

———. 1991. *Learning to Learn in a Second Language.* Portsmouth, NH: Heinemann.

Glasswell, K., J. M. Parr, and S. McNaughton. 2003. "Four Ways to Work Against Yourself when Conferencing with Struggling Writers." *Language Arts* 80: 291–98.

Glazer, S. M. 1994. "A Meaningful Way to Assess Spelling." *Teaching K–8* (April): 87–88.

Graham, S., and K. R. Harris. 1997. "It Can Be Taught, But Does Not Develop Naturally: Myths and Realities in Writing Instruction." *School Psychology Review* 26: 414–24.

Graham, S., K. Harris, B. Fink-Chorzempa, and C. MacArthur. 2003. "Primary Grade Teachers' Instructional Adaptations for Struggling Writers: A National Survey." *Journal of Educational Psychology* 73: 279–92.

Graham, S., K. Harris, and L. Larsen. 2001. "Prevention and Intervention of Writing Difficulties for Students with Learning Disabilities." *Learning Disabilities: Research and Practice* 16: 74–84.

Graham, S., K. R. Harris, and C. A. MacArthur. 1993. "Improving the Writing of Students with Learning Problems: Self-Regulated Strategy Development." *School Psychology Review* 22: 656–70.

Graham, S., K. R. Harris, C. A. MacArthur, and S. Schwartz. 1991. "Writing and Writing Instruction for Students with Learning Disabilities: Review of Research Programs." *Journal of Learning Disabilities* 14: 89–114.

Graham, S., K. Harris, and G. Troia. 2000. "Self-Regulated Strategy Development Revisted: Teaching Writing Strategies to Struggling Writers." *Topics in Language Disorders* 20: 1–14.

Graves, D. H. 1994. *A Fresh Look at Writing*. Portsmouth, NH: Heinemann.

———. 1983. *Teachers and Children at Work*. Portsmouth, NH: Heinemann.

———. 1979. "What Children Show Us About Revision." *Language Arts* 56: 312–19.

Halliday, M. A. 1989. *Spoken and Written Language*. New York: Oxford University Press.

Hansen, J. 2003. "The Language Arts Interact." In *Handbook of Research on the Teaching of English Language Arts*, edited by J. Flood, D. Lapp, J. R. Squire, and J. Jensen, 1026–34. Mahwah, NJ: Erlbaum.

Harper, L. 1997. "The Writer's Toolbox: Five Tools for Active Revision Instruction." *Language Arts* 74: 193–200.

Harste, J., V. A. Woodward, and C. L. Burke. 1984. *Language Stories and Literacy Lessons*. Portsmouth, NH: Heinemann.

Hindley, J. 1998. *Writing Mini-Lessons*. York, ME : Stenhouse Publishers. Videorecording.

Hodges, R. E. 2003. "The Conventions of Writing." In *Handbook of Research on the Teaching of English Language Arts,* edited by J. Flood, D. Lapp, J. R. Squire, and J. Jensen, 1052–63. Mahwah, NJ: Erlbaum.

Hoewisch, A. 2001. " 'Do I Have a Princess in My Story?' Supporting Children's Writing of Fairy Tales." *Reading and Writing Quarterly* 17: 249–77.

Hughes, M., and D. Searle. 1997. *The Violent E and Other Tricky Sounds: Learning to Spell from Kindergarten Through Grade 6.* Portland, ME: Stenhouse.

Hurley, S. R., and J. V. Tinajero. 2001. *Literacy Assessment of Second Language Learners.* New York: Allyn and Bacon.

Jansson, T. 1962. "Cedric." In *Tales from Moominvalley* (T. Warburton, Trans.), 150–61. New York: Farrar, Strauss, Giroux.

King, M., and V. Rentell. 1979. "Toward a Theory of Early Writing Development." *Research in the Teaching of English* 13: 243–53.

Knapp, P., and Watkins, M. 2005. *Genre, Text, Grammar: Technologies for Teaching and Assessing Writing.* Sydney, Australia: University of South Wales Press.

Labbo, L. D., J. V. Hoffman, and N. L. Roser. 1995. "Ways to Unintentionally Make Writing Difficult." *Language Arts* 72: 164–70.

Lasky, K. 1983. *Sugaring Time.* New York: Aladdin Books.

Luke, A., and P. Freebody. 1997. "The Social Practices of Reading." In *Constructing Critical Literacies: Teaching and Learning in Textual Practice*, edited by S. Muspratt, A. Luke, and P. Freebody, 185–226. Cresskill, NJ: Hampton Press.

Manzo, K. 2003. "NAEP Writing Scores Improve, But Not for Seniors." *Education Week* 3.

Marten, S., and J. Spielman. 2005. "Modified Descriptive Review as a Tool for Reflection and Professional Inquiry." *Language Arts* 82 (6): 452–61.

Martin, B., and Carle, E. 1996. *Brown Bear, Brown Bear, What Do You See?* New York: Holt.

Massachusetts Department of Education. 2001. *Massachusetts English Language Arts Curriculum Framework.* Malden, MA: Author.

Massachusetts Department of Elementary and Secondary Education. 2007. *English Language Arts Test Items*. Retrieved on December 8, 2008 from www.doe.mass.edu/mcas/2007/release/default.html.

McKee, D. 1989. *Elmer*. New York: HarperCollins.

McKeown, M. G., R. Hamilton, L. Kucan, and I. L. Beck. 1997. *Questioning the Author: An Approach for Enhancing Student Engagement with Text*. Newark, DE: International Reading Association.

McPhail, G. 2008. *Finding Freedom as a Writer: Genre, Gender and Identity in a First Grade Writers' Workshop*. Doctoral Dissertation, Boston College.

Menzel, P., and F. D'Aluisio. 2007. *Hungry Planet: What the World Eats*. Berkeley, CA: Ten Speed Press.

Monahan, R. B., and R. Henken. 2003. "On the Lookout for Language: Children as Language Detectives." *Language Arts* 80 (3): 206–14.

Munsch, R. 1986. *Paperbag Princess*. New York: Scholastic.

Murphy, S., and C. Dudley-Marling. 2000. "Editors' Pages." *Language Arts* 77: 200–201.

National Center for Educational Statistics (NCES). 2002. *The Nation's Report Card*. Washington, DC: Author.

Newkirk, T. 2002. *Misreading Masculinity: Boys, Literacy, and Popular Culture*. Portsmouth, NH: Heinemann.

Newman, J. 1983. "On Becoming a Writer: Child and Teacher." *Language Arts* 60: 860–70.

Noble, T. H., and S. Kellogg. 1992. *The Day Jimmy's Boa Ate the Wash*. New York: Puffin.

Northwest Regional Educational Laboratory. n.d. *6+1 Trait Writing Scoring Continuum*. Retrieved at www.nwrel.org/assessment /pdfRubrics/6plus1traits.PDF.

Oakes, J. 2005. *Keeping Track: How Schools Structure Inequality*, 2d ed. New Haven, CT: Yale University Press.

O'Malley, J. M., and L. V. Pierce. 1996. *Authentic Assessment for English Language Learners, Practical Approaches for Teachers*. New York: Addison-Wesley.

Perry, N., and L. Drummond. 2002. "Helping Young Students Become Self-Regulated Researchers and Writers." *The Reading Teacher* 56: 298–310.

Ray, K. W., and L. Cleaveland. 2005. *The Teaching Behind "About the Authors": How to Support Our Youngest Writers.* Portsmouth, NH: Heinemann. DVD.

Rhodes, L. 1992. *Literacy Assessment: A Handbook of Instruments.* Portsmouth, NH: Heinemann.

Rhodes, L. K., and C. Dudley-Marling. 1996. *Readers and Writers with a Difference: A Holistic Approach to Teaching Struggling Readers and Writers.* Portsmouth, NH: Heinemann.

Richgels, D. J. 2001. "Invented Spelling, Phonemic Awareness, and Reading and Writing Instruction." In *Handbook of Early Literacy Research,* edited by S. B. Neuman and D. K. Dickinson, 142–55. New York: Guilford Press.

Schleppegrell, M. 2007. *The Language of Schooling: A Functional Linguistics Perspective.* Mahwah, NJ: Lawrence Erlbaum Publishers.

Schleppegrell, M. J., and A. L. Go. 2007. "Analyzing the Writing of English Learners: A Functional Approach." *Language Arts* 84: 529–38.

Scieszka, J., and L. Smith. 1996. *The True Story of the Three Little Pigs.* New York: Puffin.

Shaughnessy, M. 1977. *Errors and Expectations: A Guide for the Teacher of Basic Writing.* New York: Oxford University Press.

Silliman, E. R, T. L. Jimerson, and L. C. Wilkinson. 2000. "A Dynamic Systems Approach to Writing Assessment in Students with Language Learning Problems." *Topics in Language Disorders* 45–64.

Smith, F. 1982. *Writing and the Writer.* New York: Holt, Rinehart and Winston.

———. 1981. "Myths of Writing." *Language Arts* 58: 792–98.

Snowball, D., and F. Bolton. 1999. *Spelling K–8: Planning and Teaching.* Portland, ME: Stenhouse.

Spaulding, C. L. 1989. "Understanding Ownership and the Unmotivated Writer." *Language Arts* 66: 414–22.

Stefanakis, E. H. 2001. *Multiple Intelligences and Portfolios: A Window into the Learner's Mind.* Portsmouth, NH: Heinemann.

Sudol, D., and P. Sudol. 1991. "Another Story: Putting Graves, Calkins, and Atwell into Practice and Perspective." *Language Arts* 68: 292–300.

Taberski, S. 2000. *On Solid Ground: Strategies for Teaching Reading K–3*. Portsmouth, NH: Heinemann.

Templeton, S. 2003. "Spelling." In *Handbook of Research on the Teaching of English Language Arts,* edited by J. Flood, D. Lapp, J. R. Squire, and J. Jensen, 738–51. Mahwah, NJ: Erlbaum.

Tompkins, G. E. 2002. "Struggling Readers Are Struggling Writers, Too." *Reading and Writing Quarterly* 18: 175–93.

Turbill, J. 2000. "Developing a Spelling Conscience." *Language Arts* 77: 209–17.

Wilde, S. 1991. *You Kan Red This! Spelling and Punctuation for Whole Language Classrooms, K–6*. Portsmouth, NH: Heinemann.

Wilson, L. 2002. *Reading to Live: How to Teach Reading for Today's World*. Portsmouth, NH: Heinemann.

Wollman-Bonilla, J. E. 2004. "Principled Teaching to(wards) the Test? Persuasive Writing in Two Classrooms." *Language Arts* 81: 502–11.

Wray, D., and Lewis, M. 1997. "An Approach to Factual Writing." *The Australian Journal of Language and Literacy* 2: 20. Retrieved on December 8, 2008 from www.readingonline.org/articles/art_index.asp?HREF=/articles/writing/index.html.

Youngs, S., and Barone, D. 2007. *Writing Without Boundaries: What's Possible when Students Combine Genres*. Portsmouth, NH: Heinemann.

Zecker, L. B., C. C. Pappas, and S. Cohen. 1998. "Finding the 'Right Measure' of Explanation for Young Latina/o Writers." *Language Arts* 76: 49–56.

Study Guide

Chapter One

The overriding goal for writing instruction in elementary classrooms is *to push all students to write effectively for as wide a range of purposes and for as wide a range of audiences as possible.* The purpose of the following activity is to explore the variety of purposes and audiences for an array of texts and consider how to include students in instructional conversations that challenge their academic proficiency and are grounded, authentic, and meaningful.

Collect "touchstone" texts (e.g., emails, text messages, story books, magazine or news articles, recipes, web pages, journal entries, etc.) that illustrate one or more purposes. With colleagues (or students) role-play a simulated "interview" with the author of each text and address the following:

1. What was the specific purpose for writing this text?

2. Who was the intended audience?

Step #1

Use responses to these questions to construct a chart.

Text	Specific Purpose(s)	Audience(s)
Example: Article in *Time for Kids* Magazine, "Planets with the Most Moons" (5/8/09)	Provides information or facts on solar system, might be helpful for personal interest or for writing reports.	Kids in grades 4–6
Example: Recipe for chocolate cake	Giving directions: Provides instructions for ingredients and procedures for cooking.	Home or professional cooks
Example: Fill in your own texts!		

Source for "Planets with the Most Moons" in Time for Kids: *http://www.timeforkids.com/TFK/teachers/wr/article/0,27972,1895392,00.html*

Step #2

"Text Sets" that align with particular purposes can serve as excellent models as students prepare their own writing. For example pick one text to explore more closely. What are other types of texts that might fit a similar purpose and that might provide a text set for exploring this type of writing with your students?

1. How well does this text accomplish some of the following common purposes for writing: *entertaining, recounting experience, socializing, exploring a question, describing, explaining, persuading, instructing*?

2. What other texts might also fit these purposes?

3. How might you plan an instructional conversation as a prewriting activity that uses "touchstone" texts to plan a writing lesson with an "authentic" purpose and audience?

Chapter Two

Case Study: Carl

Carl is a second-grade student whose parents home-schooled him for his kindergarten and first grade years. Mrs. Mitchell noticed that Carl was trying very hard to make new friends. As part of her ongoing assessment of Carl's writing development, she made the following notes:

> During whole group discussions, Carl raises his hand whenever I pose a question. If I call on him, he often is not prepared to answer or hasn't really given the question much thought. . . . Based on several running records and retellings . . . Carl is able to decode text at second-grade level fairly fluently. However, when reading grade level narratives or discussing trade books during read-aloud, he doesn't make deeper text-to-self or text-to-text connections. He also doesn't ask questions or initiate comments about the content of what he has read. This is surprising since he seems so eager to be recognized during class discussions. . . . Carl's reading response journal entries are sparse. He's a good speller and writes simple sentences but doesn't seem to know how to discuss characters or "the problem" in narrative texts even with prompts.

Mrs. Mitchell wished to address Carl's need to fit in socially and to teach him to reflect more deeply on what he is reading as well as connect that to his written literature responses. Therefore, she decided on the following goals for Carl:

1. Scaffold Carl's involvement in partner and group work in ways that encourage him to see reading and writing as ways to become socially connected with his peers (e.g., develop strategies for group discussions including reflecting on his answers before volunteering and listening carefully to what others have to say to better focus his own responses).

2. Explicitly teach narrative story structures to help him focus him on characters, setting, plot (problem/solution), and themes that he can draw upon when responding to his reading.

Activity

Using the above information, carefully review Mrs. Mitchell's writing workshop in Chapter 2. Choose one or more components of this workshop—Minilessons, Independent Writing, Conferences, or Sharing—and develop a lesson plan that addresses her goals for Carl.

Chapter Three

The following activities will help you explore minilessons and think about how they can be used in the context of a writing workshop.

Activity #1

Semantic maps help some writers plan and organize their writing. On pages 39–40 we offer an illustration of the use of semantic mapping as preparation for writing narrative fiction. Examine the map on page 41 where Mr. Gorka models how he created a semantic map to plan a recount of his trip to New Mexico. Study his map and think of a how you might create a similar map for a piece of writing you wish to attempt. Consider how you might use this in a minilesson in your own classroom.

Activity #2

Sharing the pen while drafting a piece of writing is a chance for teachers to engage in dialogue with groups of students to write and revise their writing. Writing a set of instructions or a procedure provides an opportunity to model clear, precise language that is considerate of the needs of readers who must follow directions. Try using the classic "Directions for Creating a Peanut Butter and Jelly Sandwich" or some other activity such as "How to Make Play Dough". Reflect on the sorts of explanations and elaborations students needed to include as they created this writing as a group.

Activity #3

Children's picture books are excellent "touchstone texts" for minilessons illustrating the qualities of good writing in published texts. Consider the minilesson on character development using Choi's picture book, *The Name Jar* (pages 46–47), and the minilesson on connector words that show sequence in Cronin and Lewin's book, *Click, Clack, Moo!* (page 46). What picture books can you find that lend themselves to some of the qualities for good writing that can serve as good minilessons to writing projects in your own classroom?

Chapter Four

Writing is an inherently social activity that often includes collaboration on the construction of texts. After reading Chapter 4, try out one or more of the following activities. Record or take notes of the "talk" that occurred around the shared or collaborative writing activities. What was the nature or content of the talk? What kind of talk helped students better understand the writer's craft? What did you learn by recording and analyzing the "talk" that occurs during the writing process?

Activity #1

Try doing a *written conversation* with a colleague or a student. Make an audiotape or take detailed notes on the "talk" during the writing or reflect about the process after the fact.

Activity #2

Author sharing with peers who provide constructive peer feedback is a useful way for students to determine if their writing is effective. Sharing provides both authors and audiences with experience analyzing the effect of texts from the reader/listener's perspective.

Step #1: *Quick Write* (page 59). Pick a recent event from today's newspaper. Write a 5–10 minute response in the form of a letter to the editor or a blog entry sharing your opinion about this event.

Step #2: *Author share*. Read your response aloud and ask a colleague for questions and comments about what works or suggestions about how to make this piece more effective.

Step #3: Record the questions, comments, and suggestions. Reflect on which helped you revise. Consider how this information might help you plan a minilesson on feedback or use as criteria for a teacher/student writing conference.

Chapter Five

The goal of this study guide activity is to practice uncovering how authors identify and use different language features to make their writing effective for a particular purpose and audience. When Kobe (pages 82–83) was asked to write about his gardening experiences he used a mix of genre features but his recount was hard for the reader to follow. What Kobe needs is guidance that includes:

- Defining the purpose and audience for his writing.
- An understanding of what language he might use to create an effective text.

This activity will give you a chance to analyze what Kobe was being asked to do, how he might focus on that goal, and what language features might help him to accomplish this goal.

Step # 1

Writing for an authentic purpose and audience engages students in ways that artificial "prompts" do not. In Kobe's case, the class was engaged in a highly motivating unit creating a garden in front of the school. Most of the children had little experience with a garden and were eager to participate in hauling compost, planting seeds and seedlings, watering, and checking the growth of the new plants each day. Kobe and his friends also enjoyed using the different garden "tools" Ms. Moran provided, such as a trowel and a cultivator. After each visit to the garden, Ms. Moran asked the children to record their experiences in their garden notebooks. Think about how you might use the high interest unit to challenge students to grow as writers by addressing the following questions:

- Why do gardeners keep journals?
- What sorts of writing would you expect to find in a gardener's journal?
- How does writing in a gardener's journal compare and contrast with writing you might find in trade materials with the following titles:
  - *The Guide to Creating and Caring for your Rose Garden*
  - The TopRate Seed Catalogue
  - *Recollections on a Year of Gardening*
  - Gardening with Kids in the City
  - *Andy and the Apple Seed*
- What are some different types of writing that Mary's students might create using the information recorded in their journals?

Step #2

Think about an authentic set of experiences that might offer meaningful writing experiences for your own students. This could be a content unit that has a science, history, or literary focus. What sorts of texts might students create? How might you help them participate in planning effective texts for particular purposes and audiences?

Chapter Six

In Chapter Six you will find an example of how Kobe's writing to "recount" his garden experiences might include explicit instruction of the language features of "recount" writing. The gardening unit and notebook writing described in this chapter provide an excellent opportunity to see how a particular set of genre features can link assessment and teaching. For example, Kobe and his teacher might conference to determine the purpose and audience for revising pieces from his journal. For example, Kobe might decide to revise his notebook entry to write a letter to bring home to "recount" to his family what is happening in the garden each week. This would involve language that is personal and uses recount features. He might also decide to create instructions about "How to Plant a Garden" for some other children in the school. This text would rely more on procedural recounts, description, or explanation.

Activity #1

Based on the purpose and audience, Kobe's "recount" letter or his "instructions" text would have some similar but some different features. Below you will find a chart that explains language features commonly found in personal recounts. Based on your own knowledge, next look at some "how-to" texts (such as directions about how to plant a garden or bake a cake). Pick out what makes these most effective. Then, develop a similar chart for "instructions" or "procedural recount." Compare what is similar or different between these two genres.

Language Features of a Recount	
Criteria: **How will I make my recount effective for my audience?**	**Description**
Orientation:	My opening helps my reader *imagine* the time, place, and location of the event by telling who, when, where.
Series of Events:	My piece lists a series of events in order with language that elaborates on each event. I included quotes or dialogue to help show my point of view or that of my participants.
Conclusion or Reflection:	I don't just list the events that happened; I also share my own ideas or opinions during my recount and in the conclusion.

Language Features:	I name specific participants, such as people, animals, and objects.
	I use the past tense (e.g., *we walked, they sang, the ducks waddled*).
	I use a lot of action verbs.
	I use connector words to show when and where events happened and in what order (e.g., *first, next, later, then, on, in*).
	I include details that illustrate my key events.
	I use *I* and *we* to show that this tells about a personal experience.

Activity #2

After you feel comfortable with your charts try a piece of writing. Chose an activity that you have recently undertaken (e.g. preparing food, attending a concert, running a race). Decide on a purpose—whether you wish to write an interesting "recount" of your experience or whether you wish to provide instructions about "how to do" this activity. Decide on your audience (e.g. friends, family, or a more distant set of readers who may not know you). Develop your chart into a rubric similar to that found in Chapter 6.

Next write your piece. Use your rubric to check that the language you are using achieves the purpose for which you are writing (i.e. Is this effective for the intended audience? Why?).

Finally, think about how you might use concepts of purpose, audience, and genre features in your teaching. Remember, students are often expected to simply "absorb" these differences from their reading or writing OR they are given "templates" to fill in. Either way, they miss the chance to explore authentic writing and to talk explicitly about the different language needed for writing to be effective across different purposes. It is our responsibility to help young writers negotiate how best to write for personal and academic purposes in ways that matter to them! Rubrics, conferences, and portfolio activities that include an explicit focus on purpose and audience provide solid performance criteria from which to teach and clear expectations for students to learn!

Chapter Seven

Chapter 7 provides information that helps teachers unpack the complexity of the orthographic system as well as suggestions about challenging students to investigate patterns in the English spelling system. Arguably, students who are invited to be "language detectives" across the curriculum are ready to engage in a problem-solving approach to learning spelling and punctuation.

Step #1

Review various approaches to thinking about English spelling patterns. For example:

1. Shared derivations common to groups of words (e.g., all words that contain *graph*)

2. Common word features such as:

   - Onsets (initial sounds) and rimes (word families) (e.g., *-ight/-ite, -art/-ale*).
   - Final sounds (e.g., *qua<u>ke</u>/du<u>ck</u>, ni<u>ce</u>/ho<u>ps</u>, pri<u>nt</u>/ce<u>nt</u>*).
   - Short/long vowels (e.g., *m<u>a</u>d/m<u>a</u>d<u>e</u>, grip/grip<u>e</u>*).
   - Consonant digraphs (e.g., *ph, sh, ch, th*).
   - Vowel digraphs (e.g., *b<u>ea</u>d, d<u>ea</u>d, b<u>oa</u>t, f<u>ee</u>t, b<u>ay</u>, tr<u>ai</u>t, b<u>oi</u>l*).
   - Prefixes and suffixes (e.g., *pre-, re-, -ness, -er*).
   - Singular and plural (e.g., *dog/dogs, cat/cats, glass/glasses, child/children*

3. Structures that are related by meaning (e.g., sign, signal, signature)

Step #2

Using some of the instructional ideas provided, construct a lesson for the "language detectives" in your class. Make sure that the lesson includes:

- Words that are connected to meaningful uses of text

- An invitation to the lesson that will spark students' interest and engage them in the spirit of authentic "problem solving" as they study the words (e.g., Curt Dudley-Marling's word sorting lesson on pages 115–17).

- A focus on one of the approaches to thinking about the orthographic "system" listed above.

Step #3

Try your lesson out with colleagues in a workshop or with your students. Ask them for feedback before planning next steps. Also, try this with a focus on punctuation!

Index